# Simplified A-Z
# Christian Religious Studies
## For Junior Secondary Schools

BOOK ONE

Based on the New Curriculum

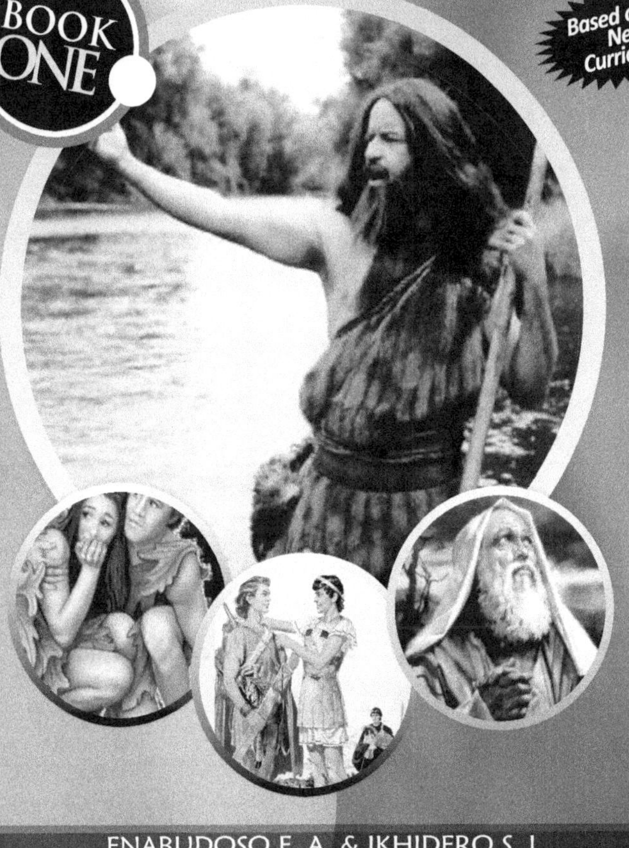

ENABUDOSO E. A. & IKHIDERO S. I.

## OWNER'S IDENTIFICATION

**Student's Name:**_________________________________________

**Date:** _________________________________________________

**Class:** ________________________________________________

**Hobbies:** ______________________________________________

**Favourite Quote:** ______________________________________

# SIMPLIFIED A - Z
# CHRISTIAN RELIGIOUS STUDIES
## *FOR JUNIOR SECONDARY SCHOOLS*
### *Book I*

**ENABUDOSO EBEHI ANTHONY (PhD, M.A, PGDE, BA)**
**IKHIDERO SOLOMON IJEWEIMEN (PhD, M.A, B.A, DIL)**

# FOREWORD

I have been privileged to read a lot of textbooks written on Christian Religious Studies meant to satisfy the intellectual yearnings and aspirations of students in our Junior Secondary Schools, but none has been so presented in unique, simple and lucid language as this one. The style adopted in its presentation is such that it will help students at this level not only to understand Christian Religious Knowledge comprehensively but also enable them apply the moral lessons in their personal lives.

Over the years, topics in Christian Studies for Junior Secondary Schools have been given different emphasis at different times with varied effects. This book offers an indebt presentation of the current issues in Christian Studies as addressed in the current Junior Secondary Education Curriculum. It is written in such a way that its use makes preparation for the Junior School Certificate Examination/ similar examinations easy and exciting. The book will help students and the reading public to have an adventurous exploit into the confrontation between the word of God and the life style of the people of today's world especially within the African situation.

The method is simple: Each unit in all the themes begins with the relevant passages of the Bible; with pictorial illustration of the biblical story. It proceeds with the exposition of the significance and the moral lessons, and ends with evaluation/Revision Questions (both theory and objective). The aim of this procedure is to enable the students to sufficiently and comprehensively understand the contents of the book.

The Simply A-Z series is indeed a new revelation in the study of Christian Religious Studies in our modern educational landscape. Without any reservation whatsoever I recommend it to the general reading public, especially students, teachers and researchers across the Country and beyond.

Happy Reading

**Rt. Rev. Msgr. Prof. J. A. Onimhawo**
*Professor of Philosophy of Religion*
*Department of Religious Management and Cultural Studies*
*Ambrose Alli University, Ekpoma, Edo State, Nigeria.*

# ACKNOWLEDGEMENT

**A** book of this magnitude cannot be accomplished without the help of the living God the source and summate of our existence. From the deep recess of my heart, I want to express my profound gratitude to my beloved wife Mrs. Zita Enabudoso and my good friend Mr. Solomon Ikhidero and his beloved wife Mrs. Joy Solomon-Ikhidero, I also sincerely appreciate the warmth and love I enjoyed in the company of my beloved mum Mrs. M. Enabudoso and my siblings; whose motivation has helped in a great measure to translate our dream of making a simplified contribution to Christian Religious Studies a reality.

I am also grateful to Rt. Rev. Msgr. Prof. J. A. Onimhawo, Dr. Mrs M. Osahon, Mrs. G. Alika, Barr. Collins Ayo, some Senior Student of Mount Carmel Secondary School (Omontese, Jacob, Pricilla and Gerald), Management of Floreat System, Fr. Evaristus Abu, who assisted us greatly in the editorial and final production of this book. Indeed your observations, constructive criticisms and corrections helped to give the work a simplified A-Z presentation.

My unalloyed gratitude also goes to the following individuals for their prayers, support and intellectual contribution; Friar Giles (Rome), Fr. Dr. O. H. Odenore, Mr. Princewill Abumere, Fr. P. Osuide, Prof. Mrs F. Iweze (OON), Srs of the Sacred Heart of Jesus (SSH), Srs of Our Lady of Apostles (OLA) Fr. A. Ebalu, Fr. Dr. F. Arhedo, Dr. & Pharm. Mrs. Enabudoso, Pharm. Mrs. Agenta, Dr. Mrs. M.I. Idumwonyi (USA), Fr. A. Ogbenbe, Dr. Philip Emafoh, Mrs. Abibatu Akhidue, Fr. Dr. A. Akhogba, Fr. P. Inanoreme, Fr. A. Obaze, Fr. Romanus Mbakwe, Thomas Ibhariale, Dr. Mrs A. Alika, Fr. C. I. Elue (USA), Fr. F. Ezechikuelo, Pastor Binitie, Fr. Nicholas Oboh, Adebayo J. Ikhidero, Edomwande Moses, Emuekhare Evaristus, Edo-Izevbuwa Eseosa, Staff and students of AB Education Centre; and the West African Examination Council (WAEC) for making use of their past questions and to all those who shall read this book. We equally thank others, too numerous to mention; we are grateful for your support and contributions, which helped in no small measure in the publication of this book.

**ENABUDOSO E. ANTHONY**

# CONTENTS

# PREFACE

From the deep recess of our hearts, we thank you for the encouragement and overwhelming patronage you gave and are still giving to the course of this **Simplified A-Z Christian Religious Text Book** since its first production to the educational sector. The overwhelming demand for the textbook and good tidings from pupils, teachers and the general public have been honestly and realistically amazing, which is an indication of our thorough efforts on the job.

As part of our motivators, we appeal for your continuous patronage while assuring you of outstanding quality and simplified text books for the student, teachers, parents and the general public at any time.

We are overwhelmed to tell you that your outstanding Simplified A-Z Christian Religious Studies text book for junior secondary schools has been **reviewed** in order to meet the current trend in the new syllabus of the Junior Secondary School. This new edition has everything you desire in a text book and second to none. The book equally contains assessment questions and a unique **workbook** that caters for evaluation of the student's understanding of each topic, and equally serves as a question bank for continuous assessment.

The Basic Concepts of the Christian Religious Studies syllabus are clearly represented in this book with:
- Adequate explanation with simple Language used taking into cognizance the level of the pupils.
- Pictorial illustration to drive home the topics.
- Quality print with clear and solid binding.
- Significance and Moral Lessons from each topic.
- Outstanding work book to serve as an aid for assessment/evaluation.

The publication of this masterpiece will be a tremendous boost to the study of Christian Religious Studies in Junior Secondary Schools and indeed, deserves a careful attention of the wider readership.

**Dr. Enabudosu E. Anthony**          **Dr. Ikhidero I. Solomon**

## INTRODUCTION

**E**very society and religious faith has an idea of a great spirit who created all things including man. This great being is worshipped by people of these societies and religious groups because they believe also that he controls their destiny. This Great Spirit who created the universe, who controls and sustains everything in it, is called God. In most of these societies, this Great Spirit is described as one of many other gods, because of the polytheistic nature of their belief. Polytheism is the worship of many gods. Christianity is a Monotheistic religion. Monotheism is the belief in only one God. Hence our concept of God here will be discussed from the Christian perspective as spelt out in the Holy Bible (The sacred scripture of the Christian faith).

## UNIT ONE: WHO IS GOD? (Genesis 1:1, Jeremiah 10:12)

God is the Great Spirit, the Supreme Being who created, who is controlling and continues to care for the world. He is the uncreated creator. God created everything but He was not created. He exists of himself. And He has no beginning and no end. God is Almighty and all powerful. His power over the physical creation is absolute, such that He can manipulate matter, energy, space and time at will. God is Invisible. He has never been seen by anyone. He shows Himself to us through His only begotten son, Jesus Christ. Christ said "He that have seen me, has seen the father". (John 14:9)

### Ways we can know God

No one has ever seen God. However, as Christians, the following are the ways we can know God;

## a) The Bible

The Bible is the inspired words of God. It is a collection of books accepted by the Christian church as inspired by God. The Bible as a sacred scripture reveals the past, explains the present and foretells the future. It thus provides guidelines for the Christian belief and behaviour. Things about God are made known to us through the Holy Bible.

## b) The Church

The church is the community of God's people. In the church we worship God, we sing praises to Him and the Priest/Pastors teach us about God.

## c) Personal Relationship with God

When we have a good personal relationship of faith with God, we get to know God better. We can achieve this by always studying the Bible and obeying God's command.

---

## UNIT TWO:　ATTRIBUTES OF GOD:

Attribute simply means a quality or characteristic of a person or being. While we cannot describe God in a comprehensive way, we can learn about God examining his attributes as revealed by the Bible. The attributes of God include;

## 1. God is a Spirit (John 4:24)

A spirit is a supernatural being, often without physical form. As a spirit, God is invisible. Although through Jesus Christ, He reveals Himself to us in human form yet it did not undermine His nature as a spirit.

## 2. God is Omnipresent (Gen. 18:25)

Omnipresent means being everywhere simultaneously. God is everywhere at every time. He is not confine to any part of the universe. He is the God of the whole world. While God is in Heaven, His throne, He is also present in every place. Proverbs 15:3 says that His eyes are in every place Jeremiah says that God is close at hand and that no one can hide himself from God (Jeremiah 23:23, 24). The classic passage about God's omnipresence is Psalm 139:7-12 where the Psalmist says that he can never be out of the sight of God.

### 3.  **God is omniscient (Job 37:16)**

Omniscient means knowing all things. God is all knowing. He knows everything. He knows the thoughts and motives of every heart. Nothing can be hidden from Him. Job said that God had all knowledge (Job 37:16). The Psalmist said that God's understanding was infinite (Psalm 147:5). The New Testament also proclaims Gods Omniscience in 1John 3:20 and Romans 11:33.

### 4.  **God is omnipotent (Gen. 17:1)**

Omnipotent means, having unlimited power. God is all powerful. He can do anything; even things that seem impossible. This means God is able to bring to pass everything that He chooses. He has no external limitations. His only limits are those He places upon himself. The book of Job (42:2) says that He can do all things and that nothing can restrain him. Genesis 18:14 simply asks, "Is anything too hard for the LORD?" The answer of course, is "NO".

### 5.  **God is Immortal (1 Timothy 6:15-16)**

To be immortal means to live forever. As an immortal being, God cannot die. He is an eternal God. Decay and death have no place in His existence. Immortality is the basic difference between God and Man. Man dies but God cannot die.

### 6.  **God is Changeless (Hebrew 1:12)**

This means that God does not change. His is the same, yesterday, today and forever. Psalm 90:2 says that before anything was created, God has eternally existed in the same state that He is now. Malachi 3:6 says "I am the Lord, I change not"

### 7.  **God is Love (1 John 4:8)**

Love is a core aspect of God's Character. Not just that God has love, but that He is love personified. The greatest demonstration of His love is in giving his only begotten son in remission from our sins (John 3:16)

## 8.  God is Holy (I Peter 1:16-25)

To be holy means to be pure and separated from evil. God is sacred and pure. He does not and cannot commit sin. When God revealed Himself to man (Moses, Job, Isaiah, Mount of Transfiguration, etc.) each encounter mentions His holiness. Isaiah called God "the holy One" more than 30 times. Psalm 99:9 says, "The Lord our God is holy" Because of His holiness, He cannot accept nor even look upon sin (see also, Habakkuk 1: 13).

## 9.  God is Sovereign (I Timothy 6:15)

This means that God is a King. He rules His creation. This is what makes Him free to do what He knows is best for us.

## 10. God is Merciful (Psalm 103:8)

Mercy is an act of compassion, kindness and forgiveness. As a merciful God, He forgives us whenever we repent and ask for His mercy. God's mercy has been defined as God not giving us what we deserve. We as sinners deserve eternal punishment away from His presence, yet in His mercy He has chosen to offer us a way for salvation. (Ephesians 2:4: Romans 5:8). Deuteronomy 4:31 and Psalm 103:8 says that God is merciful. A beautiful picture of Gods mercy is shown in the parable of the prodigal son in Luke 15.

<table><tr><td>**UNIT THREE:**</td><td>**NAMES OF GOD IN DIFFERENT NIGERIAN LANGUAGES**</td></tr></table>

God does not belong to any one nation or generation. He is the God of every people and of the whole earth. This is why different people/ Religions have different names for God. These names are highlighted below;

### The Jews/Christians

The Jews practice a religion called Judaism while the followers of Christ are called Christians. In Judaism and Christianity, God is called **Yahweh**.

## Islam

Islam is a religion practiced by Muslims the followers of Mohammed; the Prophet of Allah. In Islam, God is called **Allah.**

## African Traditional Religion

In the Traditional Religion of the African People, God is described in their different language as the Supreme Being; the Creator and sustainer of the world. This is seen in the various names for God by different tribes in Nigeria as follows;

| | | | |
|---|---|---|---|
| **Benin:** | *Osanobua* | – | The High God  (Source of Power) |
| **Ishan:** | *Osenobua* | – | God the Creator |
| **Etsako:** | *Oshinegba* | – | The Source Being who is Mighty. |
| **Yoruba:** | *Olodumare* | – | The Almighty God. |
| | *Olorun* | – | The Lord of Heaven. |
| | *Orise* | – | The source of being. |
| **Igbo:** | *Chineke* | – | God the Creator. |
| | *Chukwu* | – | The source of being. |
| **Hausa:** | *Ubangiji* | – | The Supreme being. |
| **Efik/Ibibio:** | *Abasi* | – | The God who directs the affairs of man from Heaven. |
| **Ijaw:** | *Temearau* | – | The Almighty God. |
| | *Egbesu* | – | The Great Protector. |
| **Nupe:** | *Soko* | – | The creator, who is the owner of the world. |

## SUMMARY

1. God is the Supreme Being who  created and sustains the universe.
2. He is a holy, invisible, immortal, loving, all knowing, all powerful and ever present God.
3. He can be known through the Bible, the Church teachings and personal relationship with Him.
4. Different people and religions have different names for God.

## MORAL LESSONS

1. We all must serve God because He is the controller of the universe.
2. There is nothing any man can hide from him because he is all-knowing and He is everywhere.
3. God is Holy and expects us to be Holy Just like him.
4. God shows mercy to His creatures, so we should also be merciful to those who offend us.

## REVISION QUESTIONS

1. Who is God?
2. List six (6) attributes of God?
3. Write short note on any four (4) of the attributes listed above.
4. Write the name of God in five Nigerian languages.
5. What is the name of God in your Language?

# THEME TWO:
# GOD'S CREATION

## INTRODUCTION:

Creation is the process of bringing something which was not in existence to exist. A thing which has been made or invented, especially something showing artistic talent is a creation or a created thing. The creation of the universe (world) is the divine act of God. God created the world in six days by His words; *"let there be"*.

| UNIT ONE: | BIBLICAL ACCOUNTS OF THE CREATION (Genesis 1 & 2) |
|---|---|

The Bible opens with two creation stories as recorded in book of Genesis 1:1-31 and Genesis 2:4-15. The Book of Genesis in the Bible is the book of the beginning. The word "Genesis" means "origins" or "beginnings." It sets the stage for the rest of the Bible, telling us God's plan for His creation. Genesis reveals the nature of God as Creator.

The opening chapter of the Bible begins with those words "In the beginning God created the heavens and the Earth". This summarizes the drama that was about to unfold as we learn from the text that the earth was formless, empty and dark and God's spirit moved over the waters preparing to perform God's creative world. And then God began to speak into existence his creation.

### First Creation Story (Genesis 1:1-31)
This first account of creation reveals that God created the universe and all things therein in just six days while he rested on the seventh.

The opening chapter of the Bible begins with these words, "In the beginning God created the heavens and the earth." This summarizes the drama that was about to unfold. We learn from the text that the earth was formless, empty, and dark, and God's Spirit moved over the waters preparing to perform God's creative Works. And then God began to speak into existence his creation.

1. **On the first day - God Created Light** (Genesis 1:3-5)

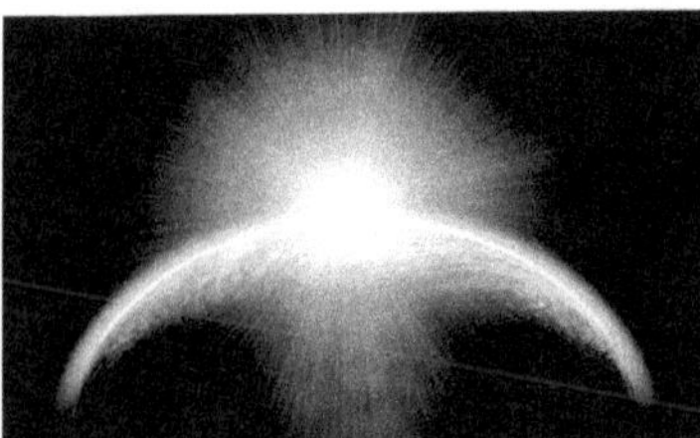

God commanded, Let there be light" and light appeared. God was pleased with what he saw, then he separated the light from the darkness and he named the light "Day" and the darkness "Night".

2. **On the second day – God Created the Firmament and Called it Heaven** (Genesis 1:6-8)

God commanded "Let there be a firmament to divide the water and to keep it in two separate places" and it was done. So God made a firmament, and it separated the water under it from the water above it. He named the firmament "sky" (heaven)

3. **On the third Day - God Created Vegetations (Land, Sea and Trees)** (Genesis 1:9-13)

God commanded, "Let the water below the sky come together in one place, so that the land will appear and it was done. He named the land "Earth" and the water which had come together he named "Sea" and God was pleased with what he saw.

Then he commanded, "Let the earth produce all kinds of plants. Those that bear grain and those that bear fruit and it were done. So the earth produced all kinds of plants and God was pleased with what he saw.

### 4. On the fourth Day – God Created the Sun, Moon and Stars (Heavenly bodies) (Genesis 1:14-19)

God commanded, "Let Lights appear in the sky to separate day from night they will shine in the sky to give light to the earth" it was done. So God made the two large lights, the sun to rule over the day and the moon to rule over the night; he also made the stars. He placed the light in the sky to shine on the earth, to rule over the day and the night, and to separate light from darkness. And God was pleased with what he saw.

### 5. On The Fifth Day – God Created the Sea animals and Birds (Genesis 1:20-23)

God commanded, " Let the water be filled with many kinds of living beings, and let the air be filled with birds" so God created the great sea monsters all kinds of creatures that live in the water and all kinds of birds and told the creatures that live in the water to reproduce in number.

### 6. On the Sixth Day – God Created the Land Animals and Man (Genesis 1:24-27)

God commanded, "Let the earth produce all kinds of animal life: domestic and wild, large and small and it was done. So God made them all and he was pleased with what he saw. The God said," And now we will make human beings; they will be like us and resemble us. They will have power over the fish, the birds and all animals, domestic and wild, large and small. "So God created human beings, making them to be like Himself. He created them male and female so that their descendants will live all over the earth and bring it under their control. I am putting you in charge of the fish, the birds and all the wild animals. I have provided all kinds of grain and all kinds of fruit for you to eat; but for all the wild animals and for all birds I have provided grass and left plants for food and it was done God looked at everything he had made and he was very please.

By **the seventh day** God had finished his work of creation and so **He rested**. He blessed the seventh day and set it apart as a special day because by that day he had completed his creation and stopped working and that is how the universe was created.

| UNIT TWO: | **SECOND CREATION STORY** **(Genesis 2:4-25)** |
|---|---|

The world was not void before God created man. There was an existing land mass, God created man to cultivate the land, this was followed by the Garden of Eden and vegetative plants. God caused rivers to flow out of Eden to water the land. They were four rivers namely; Pishon, Gihon, Tigris and Euphrates.

We are to note that in the second account of creation as recorded in Genesis 2:18, 20b-24 Man was created from dust and placed in the Garden of Eden. Though God made other creature to keep him  company yet God saw that "It is not good for the man (Adam) to be alone. He decided to create a helper suitable for him." ...So God caused the man (Adam) to fall into a deep sleep; and while he was sleeping, he took one of the man's (Adam's) ribs and closed up the place with flesh. Then God made a woman (Eve) from the rib he had taken out of the man (Adam), and he brought her (Eve) to the man to be his helpmate.

## UNIT THREE: THE PLACE OF MAN IN GOD'S CREATION

The creation of man is the climax of God's creation. God gave man dignity by making him in His (God) own image and likeness. It is further stated in Genesis 2:7 that "the Lord God formed the man from the dust of the ground and breathed into his nostrils the breath of life, and the man became a living being." God did not end there; He placed man in charge of every other created thing. He told man to give a name to every other creature. And whatever he would call

them, would be the name they will bear. The dignity of man was also established when God specially made him a companion (woman) from his own rib. All these show that man is a special creation of God.

### Why God Created Human Beings
God created man for the following reasons;

### i.  To Know Him
This entails knowing him as our creator and acknowledging him as our God. We can do this by seeking Gods knowledge through the study of the bible and worshipping him in the church of God.

### ii.  To Worship Him
God want humans to honour and pay homage to Him as He is Almighty and at all times, praise His holy name. That is why the Bible records that He delights in the praise of His people (Psalm 22:3).

### iii.  To Serve Him
It means to do what he says in a way that makes him look supremely valuable in Himself. It means to submit to him in a way that makes him look thrilling. "As for me and my house, we will serve the Lord" (Joshua 24:15).

## iv.  To Live With Him In Heaven

God also created man to live with him in heaven after his life here on earth. That is why he gave man the Ten Commandments to live by so as to be able to attain His kingdom. He also sent his only begotten son to die for our sins that we may be saved.

## v.  To Populate The Earth

God made man a co-creator by blessing him and commanding that he multiply and populates the earth.

## vi.  To Reign Over His Creation

Man was created and placed in charge of every other creation of God. God gave man the authority to reign over other created things. He does this by taking care of other creatures and beautifying his environment

## vii. To be God's Image-bearer On Earth

God created man to be His representative among other creatures. This is why he made man in His own image. On this note, God wants us to possess Godly characters that will distinguish us from every other creature so as to become worthy representative of God here on earth.

| UNIT FOUR: | SONGS ABOUT CREATION |
| --- | --- |

There are several Christian songs that emphasize God creative activities. Some of these are as follows

## All Things Bright and Beautiful
Chorus
> *All things bright and beautiful*
> *All creatures great and small*
> *All things wise and wonderful*
> *The Lord God made them all.*

1. Each little flower that opens,
   Each little bird that sings,

He made their glowing colours,
He made their tiny wings.          *Repeat chorus:*

2.  The purple headed mountain
    The river running by
    The sunset and the morning
    That brightens up the sky          *Repeat Chorus:*

3.  The cold wind in the  winter
    The pleasant summer Sun,
    The ripe fruits in the garden,
    He made them everyone.          *Repeat Chorus:*

4.  He gave us eyes to see them
    And lips that we may tell
    How great God almighty is,
    Who gave us everything.          *Repeat Chorus*

## How Great Thou Art

O Lord, my God, when I in awesome wonder
Consider all the worlds Thy Hands have made
I see the stars, I hear the rolling thunder
Thy power throughout the universe displayed

## Chorus

*Then sings my soul, my Saviour God, to Thee*
*How great Thou art, how great Thou art*
*Then sings my soul, my Saviour God, to Thee*
*How great Thou art, how great Thou art...*

## Summary

i.   God's creation took six days.
ii.  God created man to multiply, fill the earth and have dominion over other Creatures.
iii. First day: God created light and it was separated from darkness to form day and night.

iv. Second day: God created the firmament and called the firmament heaven.
v. Third Day: God created land, seas and trees.
vi. Fourth Day: God created the heavenly bodies (sun, moon and stars).
vii. Fifth day: God created the sea animals and the birds of the air.
viii. Sixth Day: God created land animals and finally he created man in His own Image and likeness.
ix. God created man from dust in his image
x. God created Eve out of the ribs of Adam, so that Adam could get a helper.
xi. God created man to multiply and reign over other created animals.
xii. On the seventh day God rested.

## Moral Lessons

1. God is the supreme creator, and He made us in His image that we may take dominion over the earth and other creatures.
2. As God's express image, we should live Godly lives and not misbehave.
3. We should create time for rest after work as exemplified by God on the seventh day.
4. Man should endeavour to accomplish Gods purpose in his life which is to know him, serve and worship him.
5. We should always give glory to God for His beautiful work of creation.

## Evaluation/Revision Questions

1. State four reasons why God created man.
2. What did God create on the fourth day?
3. Narrate the story of the creation of man and woman.

# HUMAN BEINGS SHARES IN GOD'S CREATIVE ACTIVITIES

## INTRODUCTION

God made man in his own image. And since God is a creator, man shares in the creative characteristics of God. Since man is made in the likeness of God he is above every other creature in all things including wisdom. Man also has the ability to invent item that would be of benefit to him. He also manufactures materials that make life more pleasing to him.

Man shares in God's creative activities in the following ways:

- **Scientific invention**

These include invention of cars, aeroplanes, mobile phones, computers etc. Today we see different things created by man. Man has created things like airplane, motor vehicles, computers, chairs, table, pencil, biros etc. The difference between what God created and those things created by man is that God created from nothing (ex nihilo). God does not need any existing thing to aid his creative activities; He brings things into existence out of nowhere. But man creates from things already created by God; that is, things already in existence.

- **Cultivation of crops:** Man also engage in agricultural activities where we plants, and harvest products.

- **Discovering and processing of natural resources** used in man's day-to-day activities.

- **Rearing of Animals** used as food and other products.

- **Procreation**

Procreation is the process by which an organism produces others of its biological kind. This is one major way man share in God's creative activity. This is made possible through the sacred institution of marriage. Marriage was established by God to help man advance the creative activity of God

<table><tr><td>UNIT ONE:</td><td>MEANING OF MARRIAGE (Genesis 2:22-25; Ephesians 5:21-31)</td></tr></table>

Marriage is the union between a man and a woman. Marriage is also established when a man and a woman are joined together as husband and wife to start a new family. Marriage is the foundation of the home and family. Marriage is also called matrimony or wedlock. It is a socially or ritually recognized union or legal contract between spouses that establishes rights and obligations between them, between them and their children and between them and their in laws. The definition of marriage varies according to different cultures. According to the Holy Bible, Marriage is a divine institution established by God in the Garden of Eden. Marriage is recommended or considered to be compulsory before pursuing any sexual activity.

Marriage between a man and a woman from same social group, tribe, village or clan is called an **endogamous marriage**. When a man or a woman marries outside his or her social group, tribe or village, such marriage is described as an **exogamous marriage.** Marriage is not accepted between two closely related people like brother and sister. Any such relationship is condemned as an incestuous relationship. Note also, that marriage is between a man and a woman. A marriage between same sex people (a Man and another man or a woman and another woman) is not accepted. Most cultures, especially the African culture and the Christian religion vehemently frown at such marriage.

## UNIT TWO: ORIGIN OF MARRIAGE (Genesis 2:18-24)

The Origin of marriage can be traced to Genesis 2:18 when God said "It is not good that man should be alone. I will make a suitable partner for him." (Genesis 2:18). This suitable helpmate was formed from the very rib of man and thus woman was "flesh of his flesh" (Genesis 2:22-23)." God, in this process, instituted Marriage as the pinnacle of His creation. From the above Biblical narrative, we understand that God designed marriage to meet man's need for companionship and to provide an illustration of our relationship with Him.

Marriage was also instituted by God in order for man to continue His (God's) creative activity through procreation (Birth). This is captured when God blessed them, saying: 'Be fertile and multiply, fill the earth and subdue it'" (Genesis 1: 27-28). Man's first share in the creative activities of God is in giving birth to children to preserve the human race.

## UNIT THREE: FORMS OF MARRIAGE

In Nigeria, there are three basic forms of marriage namely:
    I.    Customary or Traditional Marriage
    II.    Religious Marriage
    III.    Ordinance Marriage

### Customary or Traditional Marriage

Customary or traditional marriage is the marriage conducted according to the traditional rites and custom of the African people. It is regulated by the customary laws and practices of the people. Elders in the family and relatives of the couple are usually saddled with the responsibility of conducting this marriage.

And the payment of dowry or Bride Price is essential for the legalization of traditional marriage. Bride price here could be in cash and/or in farm produce. Traditional marriage permits a man to marry more than one wife; that is, it permits polygamy.

## Religious Marriage

This is the marriage conducted according to the rite and ceremonies of a given religious faith. Such marriage is conducted by the priest of such religion and committed to the watch of the deity (God) of the religion. In Nigeria, religious marriage could be **Christian** or **Islamic marriage**

## a) Christian Marriage

This is the marriage conducted according to Christian rite and ceremony. It is usually conducted in a church under the supervision of a clergy man (Priest or Pastor). In Christian marriage today, it is common for bride to put white wedding gown while the groom put on suit. The couple exchange rings and takes marriage vows or promise in the presence of the clergy man and their relatives and invited guest. Christianity permits monogamous marriage (Monogamy). A man is only allowed to marry one wife and a woman should be married to only one husband. The act of marrying more than one wife (Polygamy) is vehemently discouraged in the Christian religious marriage.

## b) Islamic Marriage

This is the marriage conducted according to Islamic rite and ceremony. According to Islamic law of marriage, Muslims (followers of Islam) are allowed to practice polygamy. According to the Qur'an, a man may have up to four legal wives at any one time. The husband is required to treat all wives equally. If a man fears that he will not be able to meet these conditions then he is not allowed more than one wife.

## Ordinance Marriage

This is the marriage conducted in the marriage registry or court. It is the statutory registration of marriage according to the matrimonial law in force in a state. Today, both Christians and Muslims perform the ordinance marriage even before or after solemnizing their marriages in the Church or Mosque. The Ordinance marriage permits a man to marry only one wife. A man who indulges in any extra-marital affair under the Ordinance marriage would be guilty of Bigamy which carries sanction of imprisonment.

The Ordinance marriage in most cases also involves exchange of rings between the bride and the bridegroom. And the couple and their chosen relatives sign the marriage register in presence of witnesses who may be their parents, relatives or friends.

## UNIT FOUR: PURPOSE OF MARRIAGE

### i. To Fulfil the Law of God and Demand of the Society

Marriage as we have seen is an ordinance of God. That is to say, it is a command of God. Genesis 2:24 emphasize this expressly as follows; *"For this reason a man will leave his father and mother and be united to his wife, and they will become one flesh."* Getting married therefore entails fulfilling this great command of God. Most societies place high regard for the institution of marriage. Some African societies for example see it as a taboo for a full grown man or woman not to get married. Such individuals are usually stigmatized as irresponsible members of the society. This is why most parents get worried when their grown up children are yet to get married.

### ii. To Procreate

To procreate means to give birth to new offspring. Marriage is the only union where sexual relationship is approved. This is mainly for the purpose of bringing new life into being. Any act of sexual relationship outside marriage is illegal, sinful and forbidden. Procreation in marriage is in fulfilment of God's declaration in Genesis 1:28 which says; *"be fruitful, and multiply, and fill the earth and subdue it."* In most societies like the African societies, where a married couple does not produce offspring or are unable to give birth, the families get worried. In most cases they are seen as being under a spell. Africans believe that the act of procreation in marriage helps to continue the family lineage.

| UNIT FIVE: | FUNCTIONS OF MARRIAGE |

The following are some of the important functions of marriage.

i. Marriage provides companionship.

ii. Marriage aids in procreation of children.

iii. Marriage makes couples responsible to one another.

iv. Marriage helps couples to avoid immorality.

v. Marriage helps to prevent or reduce the incidence of sexually transmitted diseases (STDs) like Human Immunodeficiency Virus (HIV) / Acquired Immune Deficiency Syndrome (AIDS) etc.

vi. Marriage brings about unity among families and different ethnic groups.

vii. Provide legal parents to children.

viii. Fulfilment of basic needs.

## SUMMARY

1. God created man specially to be a co-creator.

2. Marriage is one area where man continues the creative work of God.

3. Marriage is the legal union of a man and a woman for the purpose of fulfilling God's command bring new life into being, and avoiding sexual sins.

4. Marriage can be conducted either under Christian or Muslim rites, Customary/Traditional rites and/or Registered under the Marriage Ordinance of a state.

5. Marriage functions to discourage indiscriminate sex and avoid sexually transmitted disease. It also promotes unity among families, ethnic groups and societies at large.

## MORAL LESSONS

1. Sexual intercourse is only permitted in marriage for the sake of procreation

2. Marriage is between a man and a woman. Homosexuality or same-sex marriage is forbidden
3. Fornication (sex before marriage) or adultery can make one a victim of Sexually Transmitted Diseases (STDs) like gonorrhoea, syphilis and Human Immunodeficiency Virus (HIV)/Acquired Immune Deficiency Syndrome (AIDS).
4. Getting married when one has come of age means that one is fulfilling the will of God.
5. Marriage makes a man or a woman responsible.

## REVISION QUESTION

1. What is marriage?
2. List four functions of marriage.
3. List four ways that man shares in Gods creative ability.
4. Give two reasons why a man should not marry his fellow man.

## INTRODUCTION

**D**isobedience could be seen as a refusal to do what someone in authority tells you to do. It is the act of going against an instruction, laws or rules and regulations. It is an outright rejection of an order given by a higher authority, especially refusal to follow God's will. Disobedience was the first sin committed by man against God. Sin is on offence against God either by word or deed.

Suffering and death came into the world as a result of sin. And sin brought unhappiness to the world. Adam and Eve as recorded in the Bible were the first of Mankind to sin when they were tempted by the devil in the Garden of Eden.

**UNIT ONE:**    **BIBLICAL ACCOUNT OF THE FIRST HUMAN DISOBEDIENCE (Genesis 3:1-13)**

It could be recalled that God created man (Adam and Eve) and placed them in a beautiful Garden called Eden. In this Garden, all that man need to be comfortable was provided. God commanded man to eat from the fruit of any tree in the Garden except from the tree in the middle of the garden; which gives the power to know the difference between right and wrong.

Genesis 3 presented the serpent (snake) as the most cunning animal that the Lord God had made. The serpent asked the woman "Did God really tell you not to eat fruit from any tree in the garden?" "We may eat the fruit from any tree in the garden", the woman answered, "except the tree in the middle of it. God told us not to eat the fruit of that tree or even touch it, if we do, we will die". The serpent replied that is not true; you will not die. God said that because he knows that when you eat it you will be like God and know what is good and what is bad" The woman saw how beautiful  the tree was and how good its fruit would be to eat, and she thought how wonderful it would be to become  wise. So she took some of the fruit and ate it. Then she gave some to her husband (Adam), and he also ate it. As soon as they had eaten it, they were given understanding and realized that they were naked, so they sewed fig leaves together and covered themselves.

In the evening, they heard the Lord God walking in the garden, and they hid from him among the trees. But the Lord God called out to the man. Where are you? He answered, "I heard you in the garden. I was afraid and hid from you, because I was naked" "who told you that you were naked?" God asked, "Did you eat the fruit that I told you not to eat?" The man answered, "The woman you put here with me gave me the fruit and I ate it" The Lord God asked the woman "Why did you do this?" She replied "the serpent tricked me into eating it".

This sin of disobedience led to the fall of man. That is, the transition of the first man and woman from a state of innocent obedience to God to a state of guilty disobedience. Note that, prior to the sin of disobedience and fall of man, Satan rebelled against God, and was banished from heaven. He became the source of all evil in the universe. From this initial rebellion evil spread to earth. It is this Satan that was represented in Genesis 3 as the serpent.

## UNIT TWO: CONSEQUENCES OF ADAM, EVE AND THE SERPENT'S DISOBEDIENCE (Genesis 3:14-19)

**The serpent** (Genesis 3:14-15)
- The serpent was cursed above all cattle and wild animals on the field.
- It was cursed to go on its belly.
- It was cursed to eat dust forever.
- Enmity was put between it and man.
- The woman's offspring was to bruise the serpent head.

**The Woman (Eve)** (Genesis 3:16)

- She would bear children in pain.
- Her desire shall be to her husband.
- Her husband will forever rule over her.

**The Man (Adam)** (Genesis 3:17-19)

- The ground was cursed because of man.
- Man was to sweat before he will eat.
- He was cursed to die and return to the dust from which he was made.

| UNIT THREE: | FURTHER CONSEQUENCES OF ADAM AND EVE'S DISOBEDIENCE (Genesis 3:23) |
|---|---|

The following are the other consequences of the sin of Adam and Eve;

**i.  Shame:**

Before committing the sin of disobedience, Adam and Eve were living

a life of innocence; not wary of their state. They were naked but were not ashamed. When they disobeyed God by eating the forbidden fruit, they became ashamed and had to work out ways of covering their nakedness

**ii.  Fear:**

Before disobeying God, Adam and Eve interacted freely with God. But when they sinned against God, fear gripped them. They could no longer walk and talk with God. In fact, they had to hide themselves from God's presence.

**iii.  Separation:**

Sin separated Adam and Eve from God. They were no longer the friends of God. They now had to speak with God from a distance. Through this separation, they lost God's protection, guidance and provision.

### iv.  Loss of Paradise:

God chased Adam and Eve from the Garden of Eden (Paradise) where they had everything at their beck and call. In Eden, everything they needed to make life easy for them was provided. As a result of their sin, they were chased out into the harsh world.

### v.  Suffering:

Disobedience brought untold hardship to Adam and Eve; for curse was pronounced upon them by God. Adam now had to till the soil to survive and care for his family. Eve on her part had to go through excruciating pain in order to give birth to her children. While the serpent will forever crawl on its belly and eat sand (Genesis 3:14).

### vi.  Death:

The end result of sin is death. First, there is the **physical death**; which is the death of the flesh which everyone will now face regardless of their spiritual status. Then we have the **spiritual death.** This is the eternal separation from God.

## UNIT FOUR:   SIN AND ITS CONSEQUENCES

Sin is an immoral act considered to be a transgression against the law of God. Sin can also be viewed as any thought or action that endangers the ideal relationship between an individual and God. In Christian view, it is an evil human act which violates the rational nature of man as well as God's nature and His eternal law. Sin can be categorized into;

   a)   Original Sin
   b)   Actual Sin

**Original Sin:** also known as ancestral sin is "that sin and its guilt that we all possess in God's eyes as a direct result of Adam's sin in the Garden of Eden." The doctrine of original sin focuses particularly on its effects on our nature and our standing before God, even before we are old enough to commit conscious sin.

**Actual Sin:** is any sin that a person commits of his own free will and for which he is personally responsible.

## UNIT FIVE: SOME BIBLICAL EXAMPLES OF SIN AND ITS CONSEQUENCES

### a) Cain and Abel (Genesis 4:1-16)

Cain and Abel were the first and second sons of Adam and Eve. While Cain was a farmer, Abel was a skilled shepherd who took care of the family's animals. One day Cain and Abel made sacrifices to the Lord to worship and thank Him. Cain brought some of the produce from the land while Abel brought the first born of his sheep.

God showed favour upon Abel's sacrifice because it was an offering that came from the best Abel had to give. This made Cain very angry and jealous. Cain lured his brother Abel into the fields and killed him with a rock. The Lord called to Cain asking for Abel his brother and he said *"I do not know, am I my brother's keeper? (Genesis 4:9)"*

After Cain lies about killing his brother, God cursed Cain for killing his brother. God declared that if Cain tilled the ground, it will no longer produce food. He said Cain would henceforth be a fugitive and vagabond. God placed a mark on Cain's head and did promise Cain that no one would kill him. Cain

wandered away from the presence of God and dwelt in the land of Nod, east of Eden. The story of Cain and Abel teaches us how jealousy, bitterness and anger can destroy us.

### b) The time of Noah (Genesis 6:9-22; 7:1-24)

After the disobedience of Adam and the killing of Abel by Cain, the earth became more sinful. The Holy Bible tells us that the wickedness of people on earth became so great that God got angry with them. God saw how great wickedness had become and decided to wipe mankind from the face of the earth. However, one righteous man among all the people of that time, Noah, found favor in God's eyes.

Noah was the son of Lamech and Grandson of Methuselah (the oldest man ever). He was the father of Shem, Ham and Japheth. He feared and worshiped God amidst the wickedness of the world. In order to save Noah and his family from being destroyed with the wicked people of the world, **God told Noah to construct an ark made of *Gopher* wood** with rooms in it. He was to cover it inside and outside with pitch (a

black substance obtained from Tar) to serve as water proof. The ark should be Three Hundred cubits long, fifty cubits in width and thirty cubits in height. God instructed Noah to enter into the ark with his wife, his three sons with their wives. He also asked him to bring into the ark two of all living creatures, both male and female, and seven

pairs of all the clean animals, along with every kind of food to be stored for the animals and his family while on the ark. Noah obeyed everything God commanded him to do. After they entered the ark, rain fell on the earth for a period of forty days and nights. The waters flooded the earth for a hundred and fifty days, and every living thing on the face of the earth was wiped out. As the waters receded, the ark came to rest on the mountains of *Ararat*. Noah and his family continued to wait for almost eight more months while the surface of the earth dried out. Finally after an entire year, God invited Noah to come out of the ark. Noah's family and every creature in the ark survived the flood. Noah was six hundred years old when the flood came.

## c. The Tower Of Babel (Genesis 11:1-9)

A tower is a tall, narrow building that either stands alone or forms part of another building such as a church or castle. Babel means a confused noise made by a number of voices.

After the flood, Noah's Children multiplied and populated the earth. They all settled in a place called Shinar in Babylon, one of the cities founded by Nimrod according to Genesis 10:9-10. Up until this point in the Bible, the whole world had one language, meaning there was one common speech for all people. Over the years, they became proud and over ambitious that they decided to build a city with a tower that would reach to heaven. By building the tower they wanted to;

- see what heaven looks like;
- make a name for themselves;
- and also prevent the people from being scattered (Genesis 11:4).

Obviously, the goal of the people was not to glorify God and lift up his name but to build a name for themselves. In Genesis 9:1, God told humankind: *"Be fruitful and multiply, and fill the earth."* God wanted people to spread out and fill the whole earth. By building the tower, the people were ignoring God's clear instructions.

God observed what a powerful force their unity of purpose created. As a result, he confused their language, causing them to speak many different languages so they would not understand each other. By doing this, God thwarted their plans. He also forced the people of the city to scatter all across the face of the earth.

**Ways in Which We Disobey God**

Disobedience as we have seen is doing what you are told not to do. This, in the sight of God is a sin. It could be in various ways as outlined below;

1. We sin by doing thing which God's word plainly forbids us to do. For example it is a sin for anyone to indulge in fornication, idolatry or to be Jealous etc.

2. We fall into sin by failing to do good when we have the opportunity to do so. James said, "Whosoever knows what is right to do and fails to do it, is a sinner" (James4:17).
3. We also sin when we fail to obey the laws of the nation. For examples when the law says one should not cheat in examinations, anyone who does so has sinned against the laws of God.
4. We also sin against God unknowingly through our words, thoughts and action.

## UNIT SIX: DISOBEDIENCE TO NATIONAL LAWS

In a nation, rules and regulations are put in place to co-ordinate people's behaviours. Disobedience to these rules and regulation goes with punishment; which range from fines, imprisonment to death sentence. Despite these rules and punishments, youths of this country still disobey the law of Nigeria. Youths engages in bad practice like, stealing, Examination malpractice, Kidnapping, Fraud, and Rape etc.

## UNIT SEVEN: LEARNERS DISOBEDIENCE AND CONSEQUENCES

This occurs when learners (Students) break the school's code of conduct (rules and regulations). Every school has its code of conduct which are made known to all students. They are meant to guide the conduct of the learners while in school. Learner's disobedience is not treated lightly. When a learner disobeys the school rules and regulation, he or she is severely punished by the school's authority. The punishment received varies depending on the gravity of the offence committed by the learner. Some of learner's disobedience include:

- Failure to put on the specified school uniforms.
- Failure to dress properly.
- Lateness to school.
- Fighting in school.
- Loitering during school hours.
- Cheating during examination etc.

The punishment ranges from different duration of suspension to expulsion from school.

## SUMMARY

i.   Disobedience is the failure or refusal to obey instructions, laws or rules and regulations.
ii.  Adam and Eve were the first of mankind to disobey God which brought suffering into the world.
iii. Disobedience to God is a sin and any time one sins there are always consequences.
iv.  In our world today, the common act of disobedient to the law of the nation include: examination malpractice, cultism, stealing, fraud, kidnapping etc.

## MORAL LESSONS

1. We must not disobey God because it is a sin.
2. We will be punished just like Adam and Eve if we sin.
3. We should pray to God to help us to overcome temptation to sin.
4. We should not be jealous, because it can lead us to commit sin.
5. Whoever kills his fellow human being would be severely punished.
6. God knows and reward those who faithfully serve him as he did to Noah.

## Evaluation / Revision Questions

1. What is sin?
2. Explain the term disobedience.
3. Who were the first of mankind to disobey God?
4. Mention the consequences of disobedience.
5. What was Cain's punishment after he had killed his brother Abel?
6. State three act of disobedience common among;
i.   Nigerian youth.
ii.  Students.

# THEME FIVE:
# RECONCILIATION

## UNIT ONE: INTRODUCTION

Reconciliation is about restoring the right relationship between people who have been enemies. It could also be seen as restoration of friendship after a period of disagreement or misunderstanding. It also means the act of causing two people or groups to become friendly again after an argument or disagreement. : Replacement of a broken relationship with a new one.

## UNIT TWO: CONDITIONS NECESSARY FOR RECONCILIATION

For there to be true reconciliation, the following conditions must be met.

1) We must be ready to admit our mistakes and wrong doing.
2) We are to pray before initiating reconciliation.
3) We must be ready to forgive ourselves.
4) The people involved in settling the dispute or disagreement must play fair.
5) We must be ready to accept the judgment which is aimed at reconciliation.
6) We must be ready to apologise to the person we have offended.

## UNIT THREE: THE STORY OF THE PRODIGAL SON (LUKE 15:11-32)

A man had two sons, and the younger asked his father to give him the share of property belonging to him, while the father was yet alive. The father obliged him and the young man took his share, travelled to a distant town where he squandered it in reckless living. It happened that there was a great 

famine in that land. Having no more money, he began a job of feeding pigs. Things were still so difficult for him that he desired to feed together with the pigs. However, one day, he realized himself and decided to go back to his father to ask for forgiveness instead of dying of hunger in a foreign land.

Seeing his son while he was still far off, the father ran and embraced him, kissed him and was very happy to see his presumed lost son. He declared to his servants "Bring quickly the best robe and put it on him and put a ring on his finger and shoes on his feet; bring the fatted calf and kill it and let us eat and make merry; for this son of mine was dead and is alive, he was lost and is found" (Luke 15:22-24).

When the elder brother was returning home from the field and saw what happened, he became unhappy because his father had never organized such a big party for him. His father called him and said to him, "Son, you are always with me, and all that I have is yours. It was fitting to make merry and be glad, for your brother was dead and is alive; he was lost and is found".

<table>
<tr><td>UNIT FOUR:</td><td>THE STORY OF ESAU AND JACOB<br>(GENESIS 5:27-34; 27)</td></tr>
</table>

Isaac and Rebecca were happily married and had twin (two boys). They were called Esau and Jacob. Esau, who had a hairy body, grew up to become a hunter, while Jacob his brother, whose body was smooth, became a shepherd. Esau was loved by his father while Jacob was loved by his mother. One day,  when Esau came from hunting, he was very hungry and met Jacob his younger brother cooking pottage. Jacob got Esau to sell his birth right for a bowl of pottage.

The agreement made by Jacob and Esau, later manifested when their father got old. In his old age, Isaac told Esau to prepare food for him so that he could eat and bless him, but Rebecca helped Jacob to rob Esau of the blessing from his father by preparing the food for

Jacob to give to his father while their father Isaac gave his blessings to Jacob thinking it was Esau. When Esau came to know about it, he became annoyed and also wept bitterly. To save Jacob from his brother's anger, Rebecca sent him away to her nephew Laban, in a town called Haran where Rebecca lived when she was still young.

## UNIT FIVE: ESAU RECONCILES WITH JACOB (GENESIS 33:1-11)

God blessed Jacob in Haran and he became the owner of many slaves, animals and cattle. He then decided to go back to his father's land. But he was afraid of his brother Esau who had wanted to kill him because he stole his  birthright. Jacob further sent messengers with gifts to Esau his elder brother in the land of Seir, the country of Edom, to beg for forgiveness for the wrong he did which led to their separation as enemies. The messengers returned to Jacob saying, Esau had already wanted to meet him and he had four hundred men with him.

Jacob was afraid and humbly prayed to God to reconcile him and his brother. Jacob was afraid of what Esau would do to him if he sees him. Jacob put the maids with their children in front, Leah with her children, and Rachael and Joseph last of all. He himself went on before them bowing himself to the ground seven times, until he came near to his brother. When Jacob saw Esau, he ran to meet him and embraced him and fell to his neck and kissed him and they both wept for joy. Though Esau had forgiven his brother Jacob he refused to accept the gifts Jacob offered him. Jacob wanted Esau to accept the gifts as a sign that he had forgiven him. He insisted and Jacob's plea touched Esau's heart and therefore he accepted Jacob's gifts to convince him that he had forgiven him.

## UNIT SIX: WAYS OF RECONCILING WITH OFFENDERS

There are many ways of reconciling broken relationship:
1) Forgive the person you have problem with.

2) Go to the person and ask for reconciliation.
3) "I am sorry" "please forgive me" "it will not happen again".
4) You can also reconcile through exchange of gift.
5) Shaking of hands, hugging each other.

## SUMMARY

I.   Jesus Christ told the parable of the prodigal son and how he reconciled with his father.
II.  Forgiveness and reconciliation of any broken relationship are necessary for peace and happiness.
III. Jacob stole Esau's birth right and received Esau's blessings from his father through the help of his mother Rebecca.
IV.  Esau and Jacob reconciled after many years of separation.
V.   Esau accepted Jacob's gifts to convince him that he had forgiven him.

## MORAL LESSONS

1. We must learn to ask for forgiveness when we offend people.
2. We should be sincere in forgiving and reconciling with our fellowmen.
3. Greed and selfishness lead to break in relationship.
4. Forgiveness precedes reconciliation. We should forgive those who offend us and reconcile with them for the sake of peace, unity and love.
5. We should learn to have the spirit of forgiveness. We saw how the father of the prodigal son forgave him and how Esau sincerely forgave his brother Jacob.

## EVALUATION / REVISION QUESTIONS

1. What is reconciliation?
2. Give three reasons for reconciliation.
3. State four conditions necessary for reconciliation.
4. Narrate the story of the prodigal son.
5. Name two things Jacob stole from his brother Esau.

## INTRODUCTION: MEANING OF RELATIONSHIP

The human relationship is the interaction between people in a society. It refers to the way in which two or more people are connected and affect each other's lives. For our lives to be meaningful as human beings there must be a level of relationship or interaction with other human beings. God created the world in such a way that nobody can live alone. People depend on each other for survival. Human relationship promotes mutual understanding and peaceful co-existence. People are connected through the following means:

i.   Family ties (Blood or biological relationship).
ii.  Matrimonial ties (marriage).
iii. Friendship ties.
iv.  Religious ties (Members of the same church etc.).
v.   Educational ties (Members of same institution of learning).
vi.  National ties (Members of same community, state or country) etc.

## UNIT ONE: RELATIONSHIP IN THE FAMILY

Family simply means, a group of people consisting of two parents (father and mother) with their children living together as a unit. It is defined also as a social unit of two or more persons related by blood, marriage, or adoption and having a shared commitment to the mutual relationship. Family could be nuclear or extended.

## TYPES OF FAMILY

The basic two types of family as noted above are:

- **Nuclear family:** This is a family that consist of the father, mother and their children
- **Extended family:** This consists of the father, mother, children and close relatives like uncles, aunties, nephews, nieces, half brothers and sisters, grandparents etc.

**Importance of the Family**

1. The family is the primary social unit of the society. It supplies the society with individuals that keep it going.
2. The family also determines the nature of the society. Bad families make a bad society, while good families invariably make a good society.
3. The family serves as a means of identification. When members of a society want to identify an individual, they do so through his family lineage.
4. Family greatly influences the children. This is why it is often said that "charity begins at home". Parents are therefore advised to lead good lifestyle as this is the best way to educate and influence their children.

| | |
|---|---|
| **UNIT TWO:** | **RECOGNITION OF FAMILY MEMBERS** |

1. **FATHER:** The male parent, who is the overall head of the family. He directs, protects and provide for the entire family members.
2. **MOTHER:** The female parent who is next to the father.
3. **CHILDREN:** The sons and daughters of the father and the mother.
4. **UNCLE:** The brother of your father or mother.
5. **AUNT/AUNTIE:** The sister of your father or mother.
6. **NIECE:** The daughter of your brother or sister. It is also refers to the daughter of your husbands or wife's brother or sister.
7. **NEPHEW:** The son of your brother or sister you can also use it to refer to the son of your husbands or wife's brother or sister.
8. **COUSIN:** The child of your aunt or Uncle.

9.  **SECOND COUSIN:** The child of your fathers or mothers cousin.

10. **STEP FATHER:** The man who is married to someone's mother after a divorce or death of one's father but who is not one's biological father.

11. **STEP MOTHER:** The woman who is married to someone's father after a divorce or death of one's mother but who is not one's biological mother.

12. **HALF-SISTER/BROTHER:** A female/male child with the same father but a different mother or the same mother but a different father.

13. **STEP SISTER/BROTHER:** A female/male child of your step father or mother from a previous marriage who is not biologically related to you.

14. **GRAND FATHER:** The father of your biological father or mother.

15. **GRAND MOTHER:** The Mother of your biological father or mother.

| UNIT THREE: | DIFFERENT ROLES OF MEMBERS OF THE FAMILY (Eph. 6:1-9; 5:21-31; Col. 3:18-21; 1 Peter 3:1-7) |
|---|---|

Every member of the family has roles to play for the well-being of the family. These roles are outlined as follows:

**The Father (Husband)**
1.  The father is the head and leader of the family.
2.  He is to love his wife and children.
3.  He is to lead the family members by example.
4.  He is to provide for his wife and children.
5.  He is to ensure that the children are disciplined.
6.  He is to protect the family from external aggression
7.  He is to be the priest of the family who leads them to God

### The Mother (Wife)

1. She is to submit to the leadership of her husband as head of the family.
2. She is to take care of the home especially the children.
3. She is to assist her husband in instilling discipline on the children.
4. She is also to assist the husband in providing for the basic need of the family.
5. She is to take charge of the running of the family when the father is absent.

### The Children

1. The children are to respect and obey their parents.
2. They are to assist their parents with domestic chores.
3. The older ones are to protect and guide the younger ones, especially when their parents are not around.
4. They are to care for their parents when they are old and can no longer work.

## UNIT FOUR: CONCEPT OF A GOOD FAMILY NAME (Proverb 22:1; Ecclesiastics 7:1)

I. A good family is always united in prayer.
II. A good family is responsible and kind.
III. A good family name is better than riches.
IV. A good family loves and helps each other.
V. A good family forgives each other their offences.

### Summary

1. Human relationship involves interactions between people connected either by blood, marriage or friendship etc.
2. The family is the primary unit of human relationship. Family can be nuclear or extended.
3. Every member of the family has their various roles to promote the well-being of the family.

## Moral Lessons

1. Parents should set good examples for their children.
2. We are representatives of our families in the larger society.
3. We should let our conducts bring honour to our families.
4. We should avoid things that will tarnish the image of our families.
5. Christians should recognize the family as a unit instituted by God. For this reason, father, mother and children should perform their obligations in order to bring stability to the family.

## Evaluation / Revision Questions

1. What is human relationship?
2. What is family?
3. Give three importance of the family in human relationship.
4. Write short note on any THREE member of the family you know.
5. Mention three role each of the father, mother and children.

# RELATIONSHIP IN THE SCHOOL

## INTRODUCTION

The school is a place for formal learning. It is where children (pupils/students) come in contact with more children in the community to build relationship and make friends for life. Like the family, the school is a very important institution for the development of human relationship. Each school has an organogram which shows relationship and positions of all members of the school.

## UNIT ONE: NAMES OF MEMBERS OF THE SCHOOL

The following personnel represent the hierarchy and duties of typical public secondary school officials.

### The Principal

1. He or she represents the father or mother's figure in the school.
2. He or she supervises and oversees the day to day running of the school.
3. He or she is assisted by one or more Vice Principal depending on the size of the school.

### The Vice Principal

Duties of the Vice Principal include;

1. Admission of new students into the various arms of the school as directed by the principal.
2. Ensure that the teachers follow the stipulated scheme of work.
3. Ensure that examinations are conducted at stipulated time.
4. Ensure that the results of students are ready on time.
5. Draw up a proper time-table for the school.
6. Enforce discipline when the need arises.

## The Bursar

The bursar of a school is accountable to the principal. And his /her roles are to;

1.  Takes record of all monies coming into the schools; ranging from school fees, subventions etc.
2.  Disburses salary to teachers and other staff of the school.
3.  Liaise between the school and the Ministry of Education in term of finance.

## Heads of Departments

These are in charge of their various departments such as Science, Social Science and Arts. They;

1.  They give instructions to the various subject heads under them.
2.  They mark the lesson notes of teachers in their departments.
3.  They ensure that the teachers in their departments follow the scheme of work and teach their subjects.

## The Class Teachers

The class teacher is in charge of a particular class assigned to him or her. Apart from teaching his subject, the duties of the class teacher also includes the following;

1.  To take the attendance of students in class.
2.  To ensure cleanliness of his classroom and surroundings.
3.  To conduct assembly when his class is on duty.
4.  To conduct examinations and prepare results for the students in his or her class.
5.  To settle minor cases of fighting, stealing, and refer serious cases to the vice principal.
6.  To enforce discipline

## The School Prefect

1.  They assist the teachers in seeing to the smooth running of the school.
2.  They ensure that there is no delay in changing from one lesson to another.

3.  They assist the class teacher in ensuring that all the students remain in class during school hours.

## UNIT TWO: A TYPICAL ORGANOGRAM OF A SECONDARY SCHOOL IN NIGERIA

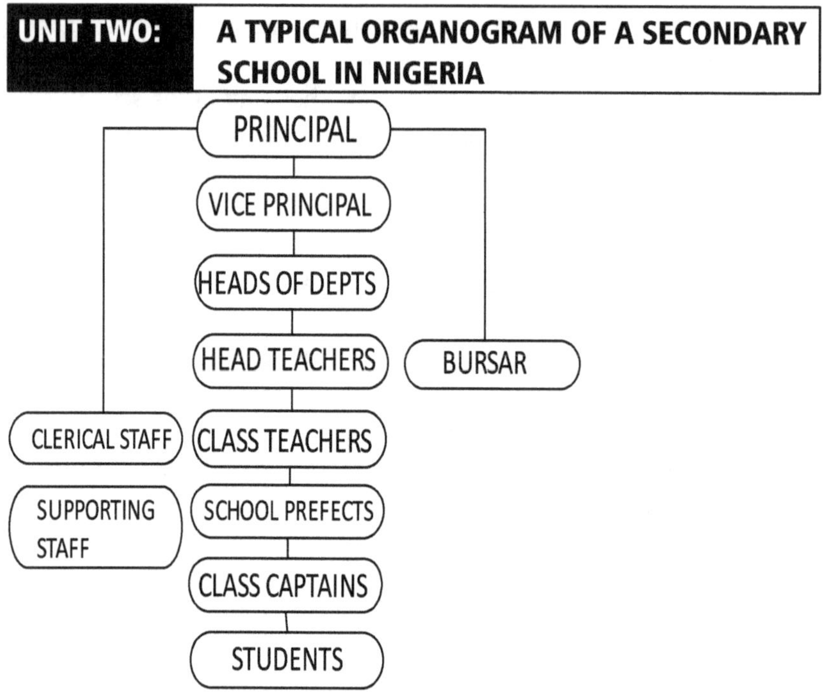


## UNIT THREE: CHOOSING FRIENDS AT SCHOOL

The school assists the family in training the child. In a school, children from different families, tribes and religion come together to learn and interact. Through interaction, mutual affection and likeness begin to develop among them.

### Who is a Friend?

Firstly, friendship is a relationship of mutual affection between people. A friend thus, is a person you know well and like a lot, but who is usually not a member of your family. Friends respect and

tolerate each other because of mutual understanding that exists between them. This helps them to relate as brothers and sisters. A friend could also be seen as a person who can take you beyond the level he/she meet you.

The bible describes a good friend as a person who sticks closer than a brother (Proverb 18:24). A friend is constant in his loyalty and friendliness, comes to the aid of his companion in distress, and gives counsel to him in faithfulness, whoever finds a friend finds a good treasure.

Everybody needs to have a friend in life. However, the type of friend one has may reveal the kind of person one is, "show me your friends and I will tell you who you are". In choosing a friend, you need to select a person who will help you to grow and not be detrimental to your growth. If you are a student you may derive knowledge from your friends who are interested and patient enough to share with you what they know. It is only from a friend that you might accept a painful truth about yourself. No matter how you wish to spend your life, a friend is an important asset. On the other hand, the way your friends treat you is a reflection of what you are to them.

## UNIT FOUR: FRIENDSHIP BETWEEN DAVID AND JONATHAN (1 Samuel 18:1-4, Samuel 1:17-26, Luke 11:5-13)

Friendship has existed from the beginning of time. The most outstanding human relationship recorded in the Bible was that of David and Jonathan. The bible said that when David had finished speaking to Saul, Saul's son Jonathan and David became best friends. Prince Jonathan thought as much of David as he did of himself. Jonathan liked David so much that they promised to always be loyal friends Jonathan took off the robe that he was wearing and gave it to David. He also gave him his military clothes, his sword, his bow and arrows and his belt.

Although Jonathan was to be king after the death of his father, King Saul, he did not hate David or see him as a rival, but he recognized that God's favour was on David. After the death of Jonathan in battle, David was greatly saddened by the loss of his friend, he cried, saying *"I am distressed over you my brother, Jonathan very pleasant have thou been unto me more wonderful was your love to me than the love from woman"*

## UNIT FIVE:    FRIEND AT MIDNIGHT (Luke 11:5-13)

Jesus illustrates the concept of good friendship in the parable of the friend at midnight. It goes to show that true friends love and care for each other at all times, both in times of joy and sorrow. Even though this parable emphasizes persistence in prayer, the message is based on the relationship involved. It tells us that a friend is;

1. Someone you believe can and will help you in time of need.
2. Someone who will still be a friend no matter how inconveniencing the demands of the friendship are.
3. Someone you can trust and depend on at all time.

### Factors that Promote Good Friendship

1. Having a level of trust for each other.
2. Love for one another.
3. Respect for each other.
4. Fairness in dealing with each other.
5. Patience and tolerance of each other's weaknesses.
6. Forgiving each other when offended.

### Influence of Bad Friends (Proverbs. 1:10; II Thessalonians 3:6-13)

Your friends don't just influence your decisions; they can alter your view of the world, change your perception and turn you into a different person. Bad friends are those set of immoral friends that influence someone to do things that are not right. The Bible advises us to keep away from bad friends; to avoid their negative influence. I

Corinthians 15:33 says that, *"bad company corrupts good character"*. So we should be mindful of those we call our friends.

Bad friends paint a colourful rosy picture of life into your mind. They show you easy ways or short-cuts to succeed. The resultant effect is that you are initiated into a world of crime, exploitation, intimidation and other evils.

1. Bad friends can lead you into truancy (the act of sneaking out of school without permission).
2. Bad friends can lead you into cultism.
3. Bad friends can lead you into smoking and drug addiction.
4. Bad friends can lead you into gambling and stealing.
5. Bad friends can lead you into fornication, prostitution, lesbianism and homosexuality etc.

## Consequences of choosing Bad friends

The consequences of cultivating bad habits through the influence of bad friends are grave. Some of them are outlined below:

1. It can result to failure in one's examinations.
2. It can result to rustication or expulsion from school.
3. It can result to police arrest and imprisonment.
4. It can result to death.
5. It can bring shame to one's family.
6. It damages one's relationship with God.

## Summary

1. The school is a very important institution for the development of human relationship through friendship.
2. A friend is someone you like and always want to be with.
3. A friend can make or mar you.
4. David and Jonathan are Biblical example of good friendship.
5. Bad friends can inculcate bad habit in you that will destroy your future.

## Moral Lesson

1. We should choose good friends that will bring out the best in us.
2. As friends we should imitate David and Jonathan's kind of friendship.
3. God wants us to choose friends that will help us to grow in the way of the Lord.
4. We should be examples of good friends to our peers in schools.

## Evaluation / Revision Questions

1. Make a list of your subject teachers.
2. Mention two factors to consider when choosing friends.
3. Give four reasons why it is good to choose a good friend.
4. List five consequences of choosing bad friends.

# THEME EIGHT:
# RELATIONSHIP IN THE COMMUNITY AND THE CHURCH
### (Matthew. 25:31-46)

## INTRODUCTION

**M**en have never lived alone. A basic requirement of man's existence has been the social bonds that unite each man to others. The closest of these bonds of relationship is the family and close kin groups. But other wider social bonds have ever been needed to link man to more extensive social arrangements. The structure developed from these more public ties has been called communities.

## UNIT ONE: MEANING OF COMMUNITY

Traditionally, a "community" has been defined as a group of interacting people living in a common location. The word is often used to refer to a group that is organized around common values and is attributed with social cohesion within a shared geographical location, generally in social units larger than a household. Community has three Dimensions:

1. **Geographical Dimension**: Communities are settlements; they can usually be located on maps.
2. **Psychological Dimension**: The people of an ideal community share a common culture: a common set of beliefs, values and norms.
3. **Organizational Dimension**: Societies and institutions within them are collections of norms and roles that govern and

channel social interaction. Community members are expected to be familiar with the entire system of norms and roles. Community leaders are on ground to coordinate interactions, promote coherence and peaceful coexistence.

## UNIT TWO: COMMUNITY LEADERS

A community leader is a prominent and respected member of a community who is perceived as the symbol of the community's tradition. A community leader governs and protects the interest of members of the community. Different communities have different leaders with variety of titles.

## UNIT THREE: DIFFERENT NAME OF COMMUNITY LEADERS

### THE BENIN COMMUNITY

The Benin's are the Edo people of southern Nigeria. Their leadership structure is as follows;

### *Oba*

The OBA is the sacred king of the Benin people. He resides in an ancient royal Palace called *Egua* situated at Adesogbe. The sacred kingship is the focal point of the Benin political system. The Oba of Benin is addressed as the Omo N' Edo Uku-Akpolokpolor within and outside his kingdom. Oba Ewuare II is the latest in line of Kings descending from Eweka. Duties of the Oba include:

1. State or fixes dates for ritual and annual festival such as Igue.
2. Create and confer chieftaincy titles to deserving citizens of the Benin community.
3. Gives the final verdict (judgment) in the settlement of major dispute.

### Enogie

The Enogie are the representatives of the Oba in smaller communities outside the city of Benin. There are two types of Enogie;

- *Ogie'isi* (Royal Duties); they are created by the Oba from sons of past Oba's they are blood relation of the Oba, he assigns them to villages which they govern on his behalf. Their titles are hereditary.
- *Ogie'Ikpanaban* (Non Royal-Duties); they are appointed by the Oba. Their titles are not hereditary

### Odionwere

The title odionwere is not bestowed on any one by the oba neither is it hereditary. It is usually given to the eldest or first (male) person who resides in any street. He presides at meetings and he is highly respected. He has the final say in cases of minor disputes involving members of the street.

## THE HAUSA-FULANI COMMUNITY

In the Hausa-Fulani community, we have the;

*Emir:* the leader of the Hausa-Fulani community.

*Waziri:* The adviser to the Emir.

*Galadima:* Administrator of the capital city of the empire.

*Sarkin Ruwa:* the leader in charge of river-related activities.

*Sarkin Fada:* the head of the palace workers.

*Madawaki:* The army commander.

*Dongari:* The head in charge of the police.

*Maaji:* In charge of the treasury.

## THE YORUBA COMMUNITY

In the Yoruba Kingdom of Oyo, we have the following chiefs in rank;

***Alaafin*** – The king and ruler.

***Oyomesi*-** (kingmakers).

***Ogboni Fraternity*** - (mediators between the Oba and the Oyomesi).

***Aare-Onakakanfo*** - (war-general).

***Baale*** and ***Magaji***, (village heads and ward heads respectively).

**Age-grades** (for special duties).

## THE IGBO COMMUNITY

In Igbo communities, though usually a cephalous in nature, there exist community leaders like;

***Eze*** or ***Igwe*** – King or ruler.

***Ofo* title holders**– spiritual consultants of the community.

***Ozo* title holders** –Chiefs.

## WAYS OF SUSTAINING RELATIONSHIP IN THE COMMUNITY

Relationship in the community can be sustained in the following ways;

i.   Respecting the elders and leaders of the community.
ii.  Obeying the laws of the community.
iii. Attending Community/street meetings.
iv.  Participating in age-grade ceremonies.
v.   Participating in community development programmes.
vi.  Being kind to your neighbours,
vii. Rendering help to the sick, underprivileged, elderly etc. in the community.

## Summary

1. A community is a group of interacting people living in a common location and sharing common values.
2. Different communities have different names or titles for their leaders.
3. Community relationship is sustained by abiding by community rules and regulations, respecting our elders and leaders and participating in community development service.

## Moral Lessons

1. We should respect and pray for our community leaders.
2. We must contribute our quota towards the development of our communities.
3. We should obey our community rules and regulations.
4. We should respect our elders and help the needy in our communities.

## Evaluation/Revision Questions

1. What is community?
2. List any three Hausa-Fulani community leaders.
3. Who is an *Odionwere* in Benin community?
4. Find out the names of your community leaders?

## UNIT FOUR: RELATIONSHIP IN THE CHURCH

The Church is the assembly of Christian faithful for purpose of worshipping God. It could also mean a local place of worship for all believers who are followers Jesus Christ. There are five key elements that should characterize our relationship as Christians;

1. **Loving our Christian Brothers and Sisters**(Matthew 5:44-47; John 13:34-35, Romans 12:9-21)

Love is the complete and unconditional acceptance of each other as brother and sisters in Christ. It is a part of the fruit of the spirit. Christians require a high degree of love to be able to relate cordially and peacefully with one another. Christian love should extend beyond the Christian brotherhood to all people. Our relationship in church is strengthened and maintained through love, forgiveness, faithfulness, self-control and care for one another.

## 2. Compassion (Luke 17:11-19)

As members of the Christian assembly (Church) we should be responsive to the needs of others. Christians should care for one another, especially the needy among them. Jesus emphasizes care for the needy as a key requirement for accepting people on the Judgment day. Just as Christ showed mercy, we should be merciful enough to show concern for the needs of the sick, hungry or downtrodden.

## 3. Courteous

As Christians, we should relate courteously with each other. We should be willing to encourage one another, rejoice in each other's success and should not be jealous of one another.

## 4. Harmony

Members of the church should be of one mind with the same goals. They should live in peace with one another.

## 5. Tenderheartedness

Christians should be sensitive and caring towards one another

## Christian Living among Non-Christian Community

In the community of non-Christians, Christians should live lives worthy of emulation. Matthew 5:13-16 aptly captions that Christians are:

- "the salt of the earth"
- "the light of the world"
- "a city set on a hill that cannot be hidden"

This means that Christians should be role models, they should spread the gospel of God's goodness not just in words but in the way they live their lives. Christians should express the virtues of love, peace, unity, friendship, honesty, generosity, tolerance, endurance, discipline, forgiveness et cetera. They must show all these virtue in their dealing with their fellow Christians and non-Christians alike. This, according to 1 Peter 2:12 will help then win more souls for Christ.

**Attitude of Christians, to Persecution**
Persecution is the maltreatment of an individual or group of people on the basis of their belief, race or social status. Most often, people of a different faith would want to resist Christian belief by any mean. In your country, some group may be persecuting Christians. However, the Bible in 1 Peter 3:13-17 urges Christians not to revenge any harm done to them. God Himself will take the vengeance. Jesus even demanded that we should love our enemies (Matthew 5:38-48).

**Summary**
1. Christians should express the example of Christ's love in their relationship with one other in church.
2. Christians should be model of God's goodness to non-Christians.
3. Christians should not retaliate in times of persecution.

**Moral Lesson**
1. As Christians, we should be shining examples everywhere.
2. As Christians we should leave vengeance for God.
3. As followers of Christ, we should express Christ-like attributes.

**Evaluation / Revision Questions**
1. Define the term, Church.
2. How should Christians maintain good relationship in the Church?
3. What does the Bible mean when it says "Christians are Light of the world"?

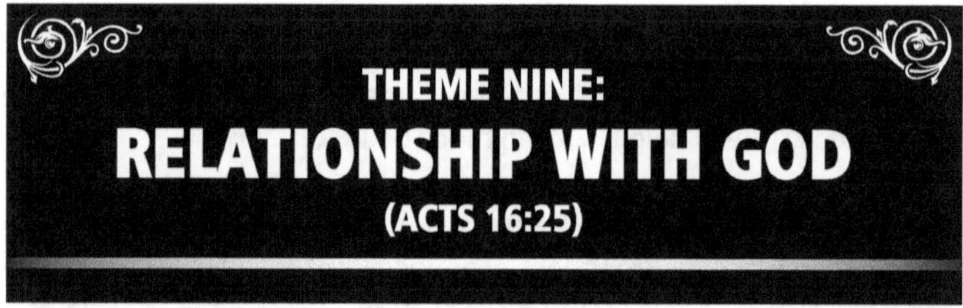



## UNIT ONE:  MEANING OF PRAYER

**P**rayer refers to communication between man/woman with God. Prayer could also be seen as the raising up of our mind and hearts to God. In prayer, total attentiveness of mind and heart is required. Knowing the relevance of prayer, Jesus taught his disciples how to make an acceptable prayer. He taught them not to pray like the hypocrites who usually pray in open places so that people could see them praying. He said when you pray, go into your room and shut the door and pray to your father in secret and your father who sees in secret will reward you. Jesus taught His disciples to pray. The prayer that Jesus taught His disciples is called the Lord's Prayer.

## UNIT TWO:  THE LORD'S PRAYER:

Our father who art in heaven,
Hallowed be thy name,
Thy kingdom come,
Thy will be done on earth as it is in heaven,
Give us this day our daily bread,
And forgive us our debts,
As we also have forgiven our debtors,
And lead us not into temptation,
But deliver us from evil.

## TYPES OF PRAYER

We have various types of prayer
- ❖ Prayer of Adoration
- ❖ Prayer of Supplication
- ❖ Prayer of Intercession
- ❖ Prayer of Faith

* ❖ Prayer of Praise and Thanksgiving
* ❖ Prayer of forgiveness
* ❖ Prayer of Contemplation

The Bible talks about different types of prayer. Knowing what type of prayer to pray and when to pray it is very important to our prayer life. In practice, we all use different types of prayer during our prayer times, and there is no reason while we cannot apply any of these types of prayers to all the situations that face us. Ask God to fill you with more of His love and make your prayer life richer.

### • Prayer of Adoration

The prayer of Adoration is the praise of God because of His goodness towards every one of us. We feel His goodness every day of our life. By adoring, our respect and appreciation for Him will grow. Such prayers also help us to draw closer to God. For example Jesus always adored and thank God in His day to day activities.

### • Prayer of Supplication

Supplication means to petition or entreat someone for something. It is about asking God for something. This involves a request for personal requests and desires. A passionate zeal and hunger fuels the prayer of supplication. Prayers of supplication are prayers that all Christians should regularly engage in, as we earnestly desire to seek God's face and know His will for our life. Ask God to give you a hunger for Him.

### • Prayer of Faith

The prayer of faith is rooted in our confidence in God's Word. When you are sure that what you are praying for is God's will for you, the prayer of faith can be employed. The prayer of faith is knowing God's will, praying for it and receiving it from Him. Not forgiving and doubting are the two greatest hindrances to prayers of faith.

- ## **Prayer of Praise and Thanksgiving**

Praise and worship brings us into the presence of God. Praising God in both the good and bad times affirms our faith in Him. Praise and thanksgiving are powerful weapons. They disarm the two most deadly weapons to our Christian walk: unbelief and satanic attacks. These two things are manifested in many different ways, but praise and thanksgiving is the two-edged sword that helps us fight against evil.

- ## **Prayer of forgiveness:**

In this type of prayer, we pray to God to grant us His Divine mercy in any way we have offended Him. The prayer of a sinner is an abomination unto God. So we need to always ask God for pardon of our sins.

- ## **Prayer of Intercession**

To intercede means to plead or mediate on behalf of another person. Intercessory prayer means praying earnestly for the needs of others, and seeking God's will for their life. We are called to intercede for others, just as Jesus is interceding for us (Hebrews 7: 25).

## UNIT THREE: WAYS GOD TALKS TO US

God talks to us through the following ways;
1) Through our Parents.
2) Through our Teachers.
3) Through our Priests and Pastors.
4) Through the Bible (His Word).

## UNIT FOUR: WAYS OF MAINTAINING GOOD RELATIONSHIP WITH GOD

1) Loving God.
2) Living a holy life.
3) Forgiving one another.
4) Reading the Bible.

5) Loving one another.
6) Worshiping God and doing good.
7) Daily Prayers.

## SUMMARY

1. Prayer is communicating with God.
2. Jesus Christ taught His disciples Our Lord's prayer.
3. There are different ways God can talk to us.
4. One of the ways we can maintain good relationship with God is by worshiping God and doing good to one another.
5. The Bible is God's word.

## MORAL LESSONS

1) We need to pray always.
2) In everything we do, we should give thanks to God.
3) We should always heed to the instructions of our parent, teachers and pastors because God speaks through them.

## EVALUATION / REVISION QUESTIONS

1. What is prayer?
2. Write the Lord's Prayer.
3. Highlight three ways we can maintain good relationship with God.
4. Mention four ways in which God talks to us.

# THEME TEN:
# THE HOLY BIBLE

The Bible is a collection of sacred books or scriptures that Jews and Christians consider to be a product of divine inspiration and a record of the relationship between God and humans. The Holy Bible reveals who God is, His divine message and His direction on how we should live to us. In the Bible, we can read about God's love, mercy, kindness and forgiveness.

The Bible is in fact an entire library of works in many forms. It contains history, poetry, prophecy, "wisdom literature," and stories of instruction, written over the span of many years.

## UNIT ONE: STRUCTURE OF THE BIBLE

There are 66 books in the Bible. The Bible is divided into two major sections known as; The Old Testament and the New Testament. The Old Testament contains Thirty-nine Books while the New Testament is made up of 27 books.

## UNIT TWO: THE OLD TESTAMENT

The Old Testament is a collection of selected writings composed and edited by members of the Hebrew-Jewish community between the twelfth century B.C. and the beginning of the Christian era. The Old Testament books were originally written in Hebrew, but a few passages were written in Aramaic.

The first five books of the Old Testament is known as the Pentateuch or Torah. The term "Old Testament," or more properly "Old Covenant," is a Christian designation, reflecting the belief of the early Christian Church that the "new covenant" mentioned in Jer. 31:31-34 was fulfilled in Jesus and that the Christian scriptures set forth the "new covenant," just as the Jewish scriptures set forth the "old covenant" (II Cor. 3:6-18; Heb. 9:1-4)

## OLD TESTAMENT BOOKS
### The Books of the Law (Pentateuch)
1. Genesis
2. Exodus
3. Leviticus
4. Number
5. Deuteronomy

### History
6. Joshua
7. Judges
8. Ruth
9. 1 Samuel
10. 2 Samuel
11. 1 Kings
12. 2 Kings
13. 1 Chronicles
14. 2 Chronicles
15. Ezra
16. Nehemiah
17. Esther
18. Job

### Wisdom & Poetry
19. Psalms
20. Proverbs
21. Ecclesiastes
22. Song of Solomon

### Prophecy
23. Isaiah
24. Jeremiah
25. Lamentations
26. Ezekiel
27. Daniel
28. Hosea
29. Joel
30. Amos
31. Obadiah
32. Jonah
33. Micah
34. Nahum
35. Habakkuk
36. Zephaniah
37. Haggai
38. Zechariah
39. Malachi

## UNIT THREE: THE NEW TESTAMENT

The New Testament is a collection of early Christian literature, which together with the Old Testament forms the Holy Bible of the Christian church. It is made up of **Twenty-seven (27)** different books attributed to eight different authors, six of whom are numbered among the disciples/apostles of Jesus - Matthew, John, Paul, James, Peter, Jude. The two others are Mark and Luke.

The New Testament was not written all at once. The books that compose it appeared one after another in the space of fifty years. The New Testament was written in different and distant countries and addressed to particular Churches. It was written in Greek language. It tells of the coming of Christ, His life and ministry, the growth of the early church and the book of revelation.

## NEW TESTAMENT BOOKS

### GOSPELS (4)
1. Matthew
2. Mark
3. Luke
4. John

### HISTORY (1)
5. The Acts of the Apostles

### LETTERS
6. Romans
7. I Corinthians
8. II Corinthians
9. Galatians
10. Ephesians
11. Philippians
12. Colossians
13. I Thessalonians
14. II Thessalonians
15. I Timothy
16. II Timothy
17. Titus
18. Philemon
19. Hebrews
20. James
21. I Peter
22. II Peter
23. I John
24. II John
25. III John
26. Jude

### APOCALYPSE (1)
27. Revelation

# THEME ELEVEN:
# CALL TO OBEDIENCE

## UNIT ONE: MEANING OF OBEDIENCE

Obedience means doing what you are being told to do by someone in authority. It means diligently following the instruction of an instructor. Obedience as opposed to disobedience is a life-and-death issue. God has given humankind the innate power of choice: the choice of obedience leads to God's promised blessing of life; the choice of disobedience leads to curse, judgment, and death. The obedience of Abraham is perhaps most exemplary in the Old Testament. On two occasions, he demonstrated total submission to God's will.

## UNIT TWO: THE CALL OF ABRAHAM (Genesis 12:1-7)

Abraham was born in a city called Ur of the Chaldeans. He was the son of Terah and initially called Abram. His place of birth was renowned for Idol worshiping. Indeed his father Terah was an Idol worshipper and Abram was not comfortable with this. He left his father's house and settled in Haran with his wife Sarai. It was here that God's call Abram and commanded him to go to a new land (Genesis 12). This call meant leaving Ur of the Chaldeans, a highly developed city, to go to the unknown, unfamiliar land that God would show to him: the land of Canaan.

## UNIT THREE: ABRAHAM OBEYS GOD'S CALL
## (Genesis: 12:1-9)

At age Seventy-Five (75), God called Abram to leave his home and family behind and follow God into a strange land that He would give him. Abram took his wife, his nephew, Lot, and his possessions and departed. Abram moved south into the land of Canaan, a land inhabited by a warrior people called the Canaanites. He settled temporarily in Shechem, where God appeared to him and promised that his descendants would inherit the land of Canaan. Abram built an altar for God there before proceeding through Beth-el.

## UNIT FOUR: BLESSINGS FROM OBEYING GOD'S CALL (Genesis 17:1-21, 21:1-7; 25:1-4)

As a result of Abram's obedience, God once again appeared to him when he was 99 years old and renewed His covenant with Abram through the sign of circumcision. Circumcision means cutting of the foreskin of a male child's genital, eight days after birth. God even expanded the promises: if Abram would "walk before [the LORD] and be upright" then God would make Abram the "father of a multitude of nations." At this stage God changed Abram's name to Abraham, which means "the father of many nations," and He changed Sarai's name to Sarah, meaning "princess." God also revealed that the promises would not come to Abraham through Ishmael, (the child born to him through Hagar, Sarah's maid) but through another son that would be born to Sarah in a year's time. Abraham laughed at this seemingly absurd promise, because Abraham was 99 at the time and Sarah was 89. When Abraham laughed, God said the boy's name would be Isaac, which means "he laughs."

Abraham's obedience results in his being elected a chosen one for a special role in God's salvation-plan for humankind. Among the covenants God made with him was that;

i.   God will make of him a great nation.
ii.  God will bless him and make his name great.
iii. God will bless those who bless him and curse those who curse him.
iv.  God will make all the families of the earth through him blessed.

## UNIT FIVE: THE BIRTH OF ISAAC (Genesis. 21:1-8)

The LORD blessed Sarah, as he had promised and she became pregnant and bore a son to Abraham, and the boy was named Isaac.

Abraham was a hundred years old when Isaac was born. In obedience to the terms of God covenant, Abraham circumcised Isaac when he was eight days old. Sarah said, "God has brought me joy and laughter. Everyone who hears about it will laugh with me" Then she added "who would have said to Abraham that Sarah would nurse children? Yet I have born him a son in his old age" The child grew and on the day that he was weaned, Abraham gave a great feast.

## UNIT SIX:   MEANING OF SACRIFICE

Sacrifice is the offering of food, objects or the lives of animals to a divine being or deity, as an act of worship or appeasement. It is a religious rite in which an object is offered to a divinity in order to establish, maintain, or restore a right relationship of a human being to the sacred order. Sacrifice can also mean giving up of something valuable in order that something more valuable might be obtained; e.g., parents make sacrifices for their children, one sacrifices a limb for one's country. But the original use of the term was peculiarly religious, referring to a cultic act in which objects were set apart or consecrated and offered to a god or some other supernatural power.

## UNIT SEVEN:   THE SACRIFICE OF ISAAC (Genesis. 22:1-18)

Abraham was asked in a test of faith by God to take his son Isaac onto Mount Moriah and sacrifice him as a burnt offering. Abraham submitted, despite the fact that Isaac was his only son. He took Isaac up onto the mountain. On their way Isaac asked his  father, "where is the lamb for the burnt offering" and his father told him that God will provide.

When they came to the place which God had told him about, Abraham built an altar and arranged the wood on it. He tied up his son and placed him on the altar, on top of the wood. Then he picked up the knife to kill him, but the angel of the LORD called to him from heaven, to look around. Abraham looked round and saw a ram caught in a bush by its horns. He went and got it and offered it as a burnt offering instead of his son. Abraham named that place, "the LORD provides." For this singular act of faith, God reiterated His promises to Abraham again, at this point, and made the covenant binding as follows;

- God vowed with His Almighty Name to richly bless Abraham.
- He vowed to make Abraham's descendant as many as the stars in the sky.
- He vowed to bless Abraham's descendants for his sake.

## SUMMARY

i.   Obedience means following the instruction of a higher authority.
ii.  The obedience of Abraham to God's instructions is the most exemplary expression of obedience in the Old Testament.
iii. In obedience to God's command Abraham was ready to sacrifice his only son.
iv.  God vowed to bless Abraham and his descendants as a result of his obedience.

## MORAL LESSON

1. God blesses those that obey His words and keep His command merit.
2. We show that we love God by obeying Him.
3. God called Abraham and he answered. Today, we are called Just like Abraham to serve Him 'we should obey'.

## EVALUATION/REVISION QUESTIONS

1. Define Obedience.
2. Write three blessing of Abraham from obeying God's call.
3. Narrate the story of the call of Abraham.

# THEME TWELVE:
# CALL TO FREEDOM

## UNIT ONE: MEANING OF FREEDOM

Freedom means not being under control of anyone or anything. It is the absence of slavery, the ability to do and go as one desires. Freedom could also be seen as the power or right to act, speak and do things that you want without any one stopping you. Only God has absolute freedom. He is not controlled from the outside.

## UNIT TWO: TYPES OF FREEDOM

1) Freedom of speech
2) Political freedom
3) Freedom of movement
4) Freedom of worship
5) Freedom of association
6) Freedom from poverty

## UNIT THREE: THE BIRTH OF MOSES (EXODUS 1 & 2)

After the death of Joseph the Pharaoh who knew Joseph also died. There came another Pharaoh who did not know Joseph. At that time, the Israelites had increased in Egypt. The number was so great that the new Pharaoh became afraid of them. So Pharaoh ordered that their newborn sons be killed. What a terrible panic! Egyptian soldiers broke into all the houses and carried off the babies.

It was at this period that Moses was born. Moses was the son of Amram and Jochebed from the house of Levi. When Moses was born, to save her infant son, the mother of Moses hid her baby in a papyrus basket and placed it on the river. A princess was bathing. Suddenly, she saw the basket floating on the water! "Oh, a tiny little baby! I'll take care of you. I will call you Moses, because that means 'save from the water'".

Moses grew up. He knew how miserable his people were in Egypt. One day, he saw an Egyptian soldier beating a Hebrew, one of his people. He looked, seeing no one; he killed the Egyptian and hid him in the sand. The next day he saw two Hebrews struggling together and he said to the one that did wrong, "why do you strike your fellow?" and he answered "who made you a prince and a judge over us? Do you mean to kill me as you killed the Egyptian?". With this response Moses realized that his crime was no longer a secret, so he fled to the land of Midian to escape from Pharaoh who wanted to kill him.

## UNIT FOUR: THE CALL OF MOSES (EXODUS 3; 4:1-17)

One day, while Moses was tending the flock of his father-in-law Jethro priest of Midian, he came to Horeb the mountain of God. There an angel of the Lord appeared to him in a flam of fire out of a bush. As he looked, he saw the fire was burning without consuming the bush; he went to look at this remarkable sight. When he came closer, God called out to him, Moses, Moses. Moses answered *here I am*. Then God said, "come no nearer remove the sandals from your feet for the place which you are standing is Holy ground.

Then God said to him "I am the God of your father, the God of Abraham, Isaac and Jacob". And Moses hid his face because he was afraid to look at God. Then God said that He has heard and seen the sufferings of His people and so, "come I will send you to Pharaoh that

you may bring forth my people, the sons of Israel, out of Egypt. Then Moses asked God what name will he say to the Israelites when they ask him who sent him. God said to him "I am who I am". That he should tell them that 'I am who I am sent me to you'.

## UNIT FIVE:   DELIVERANCE OF ISRAEL FROM EGYPT

**(Exodus 4; 5:1-22; 7"14-29; 11:1-10; 14:15-31)**

Moses was called by God to take up the responsibility of obtaining political freedom for the people of Israel, he was unwilling to go as he was a stammerer. God assured him of his protection and with the help of his brother Aaron, he later agreed to lead the people of Israel to freedom.

On getting there, Moses demanded for permission for a three-day journey from Pharaoh to enable them hold a feast in the wilderness to God. Pharaoh refused; instead, he increased the labour of the Israelites in the field. Each time Moses and Aaron went to Pharaoh to ask him to release the Jews, Pharaoh refused. The people of Israel cried to God, and God heard their cries. God was angry and punished Pharaoh and the Egyptians with a series of ten plagues (natural disaster). The last plague which was the death of the first born of the Egyptian forced Pharaoh to allow the Israelites to go.

## UNIT SIX:   THE TEN PLAGUES

1.   Water of River Nile was turned to blood.
2.   Great number of frogs came from River Nile and went into the streets and houses.
3.   Lice and small insects swarmed on Pharaoh and his people.
4.   Great swarms of flies were sent to Pharaoh and his people.
5.   Diseases and death came upon the animals.
6.   Boils came on the people and animals.
7.   Thunders, lightning and hail rained from heaven.
8.   Swarms of locusts came into the land of Egypt and ate up all the plants.
9.   Darkness for three days covered the land of Egypt.
10.   The last and worst of all was the death of the first born sons of every Egyptian.

**Song of O' King Pharaoh Let my people go**

*O' King Pharaoh Let my people go;*
*Let my people go;*
*Let my people go;*

*O' King Pharaoh Let my people go;*
*To thy promise land...*

<table><tr><td>**UNIT SEVEN:**</td><td>**DEBORAH AND BARAK LEAD THEIR PEOPLE TO FREEDOM (Judges 4:1-24)**</td></tr></table>

Deborah was the fifth judge of Israel, a Prophetess, the only female Judge and the wife of Lappidoth. After the people had settled in the land of Canaan, she was Judge over Israel at the time that Jabin was the king of Canaan and Sisera was the commander of his army. Jabin and Sisera oppressed the people of Israel for twenty years and there were frequent conflicts between the people of Israel and Canaan.

One day, Deborah sent for Barak the son of Abinoam and told him what the Lord the God of Israel commanded. She told him to go to mount Tabor with ten thousand soldiers from the tribe of Naphtali and Zebulun that the Lord will deliver Sisera and his army into his hand.

When Barak went down Mount Tabor, followed by his ten thousand men, the Lord put Sisera and his chariot and all his forces to rout before Barak. Barak and his army pursued them and killed all of them. Meanwhile, Sisera fled on foot and was welcomed to the tent by Jael the wife of Heber the Kenite. Sisera said to Jael, " I Pray you, give me a little water to drink for I am thirsty". She gave him milk and drink and covered him with a rug. He said to her, "stand at the door of the tent and if any man comes and ask you, is anyone here? Say, no." but Jael the wife of Heber took a hammer in her hand, and went softly to him and drove the tent peg into his temple, till it went down into the ground, as he was laying fast asleep from weariness and he died at the spot. Behold, when Barak came looking for Sisera, Jael showed him where Sisera laid dead with the tent peg in his temple. Barak and the army of Israel went ahead to kill Jabin the king of Canaan. Deborah and Barak sang praises to God when the battle was over.

## SUMMARY

1. Moses accepted the responsibility given to him by God, to lead the people of Israel out of Egypt to freedom.
2. The last plague which was the death of the first born of the Egyptian forced Pharaoh to allow the Israelites to go.
3. Deborah was a female Judge and a Prophetess.
4. Jabin oppressed the Israelites for twenty years because they did what was evil in the sight of the Lord.
5. Sisera was killed by Jael the wife of Heber.
6. Deborah and Barak defeated the Canaanites led by Jabin and Sisera in battle.

## MORAL LESSONS

1. We have the responsibility to contribute in various ways in bringing about freedom in the society.
2. When we are given assignment, we must carry out the assignment faithfully like Moses, Deborah and Barak.
3. The Israelites were oppressed in Egypt for about 400 years, but God did not forget them. In His own time he brought them out according to his promise.
4. God can use anybody for good purposes if we are near and dear to him.
5. If we are given any role to play in the community, we should do our best to play it well.

## EVALUATION / REVISION QUESTIONS

1. Define freedom.
2. Narrate the story of the call of Moses.
3. State the ten plagues which God used to punish the Egyptians.
4. Give an account of the defeat of the Canaanites by Deborah.
5. Name five types of freedom in the society.
6. Explain how Sisera was killed.
7. Who was Jael husband?

# THEME THIRTEEN:
# CALL TO SERVICE

## UNIT ONE: INTRODUCTION

**Meaning of Service**

Service is the act of helping or doing work for someone. Service also involves assisting individuals, organizations or the society at large to perform particular task to help them achieve their goal. Every individual, especially Christians are called to the service of God and that of humanity.

## UNIT TWO: EXAMPLE OF PEOPLE WHO SERVED IN THE BIBLE

Some examples of people who served in the Holy Bible are:
- Joseph
- Ruth

**Joseph's call to service**

Joseph was the eleventh son of Jacob (Israel). His mother was Rachel. And he was the most beloved son of his father. He had dreams that depict his being a Leader. He was hated by his envious brothers who were angry and jealous of their father's love and gift to Joseph, (a resplendent "coat of many colours") and his dreams that portrayed him as their leader. The hatred for Joseph was so much that they connived to sell him.

**Joseph Is Sold To Egypt** (Genesis. 37:12-36)

One day when Joseph's brothers had gone to Shechem to take care of their father's flock, Jacob sent Joseph to see how they are faring. When the brothers saw him from afar, they said to one another: "Here comes that dreamer". They suggested killing him but Reuben intervened and told them to throw him inside a dry well which they did after stripping off his robe.

While they were still thinking of what to do to him, they saw some Ishmaelite (Midianite) merchants traveling from Gilead to Egypt. Judah suggested that they sell him into slavery since they would have nothing to gain by killing him. They sold Joseph for Twenty Shekels (Twenty pieces of silver) and went home to tell their father that he might had been killed by a wild animal. They dipped his coat in the blood of a slaughtered sheep and presented it to their father to convince their father of his death. Meanwhile in Egypt, the Ismaelites sold Joseph to Potiphar, one of the king's officers.

<table>
<tr><td>**UNIT THREE:**</td><td>**JOSEPH SERVES IN THE HOUSE OF POTIPHAR (GENESIS 39:1-23)**</td></tr>
</table>

While in Potiphar's house, The Lord was with Joseph and He gave him success in all he rendered. He was efficient and diligent in his service to Potiphar. He proved to his master that he was a godly and reliable servant by being loyal and accountable. This earned him the trust and love of his master Potiphar. Potiphar trusted Joseph to the extent of putting him (Joseph) in charge of his entire household.

**Joseph Faces Temptation in the House of Potiphar (Genesis 39:7-20)**

Physically, Joseph was well-built and handsome. This attracted his master's wife to him. After sometime, Potiphar's wife persuaded him to lie with her; but Joseph who fears God refused the temptation of his master's wife. Joseph told her that doing such is an act of grave wickedness to his master and a sin against God.

One day when Joseph was in the house doing his work and none of the men was there in the house, his master's wife tried to compel

him to lie with her. Joseph fled from her and ran out of the house but left his garment in her hand. Potiphar's wife called out to the men of the house and lied against Joseph. When her husband returned she repeated the lies. Potiphar believed the lies of his wife and ordered Joseph whom he trusted to be thrown into prison.

<table><tr><td>UNIT FOUR:</td><td>JOSEPH INTERPRETS THE DREAMS OF THE BUTLER AND THE BAKER (GEN. 40:1-23)</td></tr></table>

Even inside the prison, Joseph found favour in the sight of the prison keeper. He was made the caretaker of all the prison inmates. Sometime after, Pharaoh's Chief Cup Bearer (Butler) and his Chief Baker offended him and he put them in the prison. One night, while in prison they both had a dream and were very worried about it. They needed someone to interpret their dreams and Joseph through the help of God interpreted it for them.

**The Butler's Dream** (Genesis 40:9-11)

In the Butler's dream, he saw a vine with three branches before him. The vine produced grapes fruits which he pressed into Pharaoh's cup in his hand and gave to pharaoh to drink.

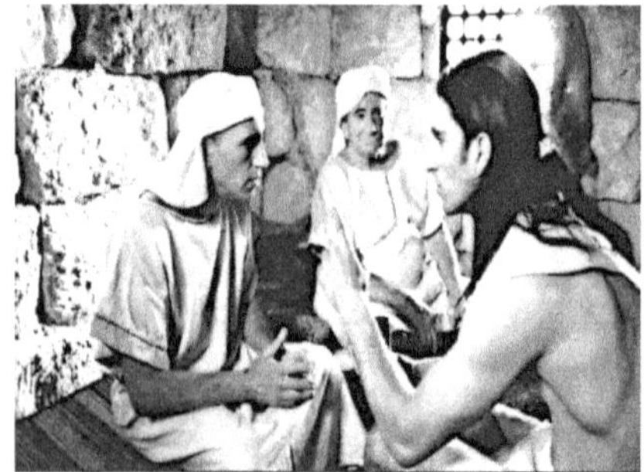

### Joseph's Interpretation (Genesis 40:12-15)

In his interpretation, Joseph told the Butler that the three vine branches represent three days. That in three days' time, Pharaoh will release the Butler from prison and restore him back to his position as the King's (Pharaoh's) cup bearer (Butler). Joseph begged the Butler to remember him when Pharaoh eventually freed and restored him to his position. He even told the Butler how he was stolen from the Hebrew land to Egypt; and that he did nothing wrong to deserve being in Jail.

### The Baker's Dream (Genesis 40:16-117)

The Baker on his part saw three cake baskets on his head. The uppermost basket contains variety of baked food for Pharaoh. But birds came and were eating these baked food out of the Basket in his head.

### Joseph's Interpretation (Genesis 40:18-19)

The three baskets according to Joseph's interpretation represent three days. In three days' time Pharaoh will hang him in a tree and the birds of the air will eat his flesh.

Indeed three days' time was Pharaoh's Birthday. He made a feast for all his servants. He set his chief Butler free and restored him to his position as interpreted by Joseph. But for the Chief Baker, just as Joseph has revealed he was ordered to be hanged by Pharaoh.

## UNIT FIVE: JOSEPH INTERPRETS PHARAOH'S DREAMS AND BECOMES THE GOVERNOR OF EGYPT (GEN. 41:1-51)

When the Butler gained freedom and was restored to his office in Pharaoh's service, he forgot all about Joseph until two years later

when Pharaoh had a dream and needed a competent interpreter of his dream.

### Pharaoh's First Dream (Genesis 41:1-4)

In Pharaoh's first dream, he was standing by the bank of River Nile and saw seven fat and well fed cows emerge out of the river. They fed by the reed grass on the river bank. Suddenly seven other gaunt and thin cows came out of the river and stood by the fat cows. These gaunt and thin cows ate up the seven sleek and fat cows, and Pharaoh woke up.

## Pharaoh's Second Dream (Genesis 41:5-7)

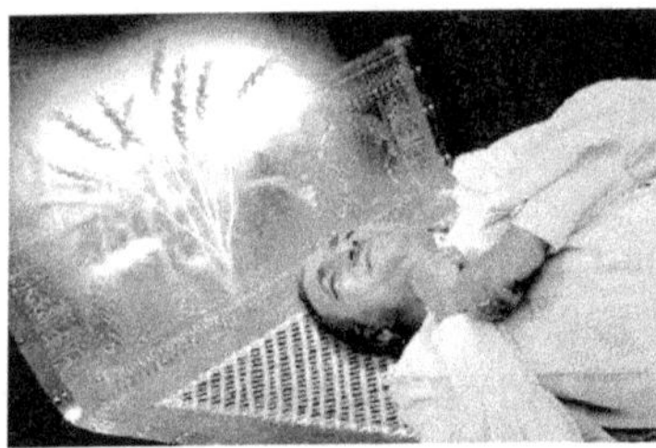

Pharaoh fell asleep again and had another dream. In this dream, he saw seven plump and good ears of grain growing on a stalk. After these, sprouted seven thin ears of grain; but the seven thin ears of grain swallowed up the seven plump and good ears. And Pharaoh woke up.

Pharaoh was so worried by this dream that at dawn he assembled the magicians and wise men of Egypt and told them about the dream. But nobody could interpret them to him. This was when the chief Butler remembered Joseph. He told Pharaoh about how Joseph, a Hebrew prisoner had interpreted their dreams while they were in prison; and how everything he said came to pass. Pharaoh quickly ordered that Joseph be released, cleaned up and brought before him. Pharaoh told Joseph about his dream.

## Joseph's Interpretation of Pharaoh's Dreams (Genesis 40:25-32)

Joseph told Pharaoh that both dreams are one and same. He said God is revealing to Pharaoh that there would be seven years of bountiful harvest throughout the land of Egypt. These seven years of abundance would then be followed by seven years of famine. He told Pharaoh that these seasons of abundance and scarcity have been fixed by God and God will bring it to pass in the shortest possible time.

**Joseph then advised Pharaoh to do the following:**

1. Appoint a wise man to be in charge of the land.
2. Appoint commissioners that will take and store one-fifth of the harvest during the seven years of abundance.

3. Ensure that these stored food be reserved to cater for the seven years of famine so that the Land might not be ruined by the famine.

Pharaoh told Joseph that there is no other wise man as capable as him to take up these recommended tasks; as the spirit of God is upon him. And since God has revealed all these to Joseph, He appointed him the second in command to him (Pahraoh) in Egypt. By this appointment, Pharaoh put Joseph in charge of the whole land of Egypt. He gave him an Egyptian name; Zaphenath-Paneah and an Egyptian wife, Asenath, daughter of Potiphera (Priest of On). They had two sons; Manasseh and Ephraim.

| UNIT SIX: | JOSEPH'S STEWARDSHIP IN HELPING PEOPLE DURING THE FAMINE (GEN. 41:53-57) |

Joseph was thirty years old when he became the prime minister of Egypt. He travelled throughout the land of Egypt during the period of plenty and diligently stored up huge quantities of grain, like the sand of

the sea. Then came the period of famine as predicted by Joseph and the people cried out to Pharaoh for bread. Pharaoh told them to go to Joseph and do what he says they should do. Joseph thus opened the store houses and sold grain to the Egyptians.

**Joseph's brothers in Egypt** (Gen. 42:1-38)

The famine was severe over all the earth. Neighbouring countries heard about the availability of grain in Egypt and they came to Egypt to buy. In Canaan, Jacob and Joseph's brothers heard that grains were available in Egypt. Jacob sent his sons excluding Benjamin to go to Egypt to buy grain (food). When they got to Egypt and brought before

Joseph, they did not recognize him and they bowed before him. Joseph knew them but spoke roughly to them. He accused them of being spies and imprisoned them for three days. To prove their innocence, he impressed them to bring Benjamin. He held Simeon bound in Egypt and gave the others grain to take to Canaan. He placed the money with which they purchased their grain inside each of

their bag of grain. They discovered this on their way home and were afraid. They told their father (Jacob) all that happened in Egypt. How the Prime Minister of Egypt had detained Simeon and demanded that they bring Benjamin. Jacob was greatly depressed by this.

**Joseph receives his brothers again** (Gen. 43:1-34)
When they exhausted the grain they bought from Egypt, Jacob sent his sons to go and buy more grains in Egypt. Judah reminded their father that they have to prove to the Egyptian Prime Minister (Joseph) that they were honest men by bringing Benjamin with them. Judah convinced Jacob their father that Benjamin will be safe in their care. Jacob released Benjamin and asked them to take some gifts with them as presents to the Egyptian Prime Minister. He also told them to take double money with them to pay back the money they found in their sacks.

They arrived Egypt and presented themselves to Joseph. When Joseph saw Benjamin with them he ordered his steward to take them to his house to have dinner with them. They told the steward how they found the money with which they paid for the grains they bought in their various sacks. He told them not to worry about it. The steward brought Simeon out to them. He also gave them water to wash their feet. Joseph came in and they all bowed their heads and worshipped him while presenting to him the gifts they brought. Joseph enquired about the welfare of their father. And he was deeply touched when he saw Benjamin, his mother's son. He excused himself, entered his room and wept because of his love for Benjamin. He washed his face and came back to meet with his brothers and served them food from Joseph's table. Joseph ensured that Benjamin was well fed. He ordered that their sacks be filled with as much grain as they can carry but that each man's money be kept back in their sack and that his silver cup be put in Benjamin's bag.

## The Missing Cup (Gen. 44:1-34)

Joseph waited for his brothers to go beyond the city and then sent his steward to overtake them. He accused them of returning evil for good by stealing his master's silver cup. They said they will never do such a thing. The steward searched from the eldest to the youngest and found the silver cup  in Benjamin's sack. Joseph pretended to be angry with them when they came back to the city. Judah remorsefully pleaded for Joseph to make them his slaves. But Joseph insisted that only the man who stole the cup would be held bound in Egypt. Judah pleaded that if they do not take Benjamin with them home, their father, Jacob would die. Joseph could not control his tears any longer; he wept so loudly the Egyptians heard him, and Pharaoh's household heard about it. He ordered everyone to go out and revealed himself to his brothers. He said "I am Joseph your brother! Is my father still alive?" The brothers were dumbfounded. He told them, "Do not be distressed because you sold me here. It was God who sent me ahead to save your lives and those of many others". He told them to go back to Canaan and bring their father and everything they had to Egypt. This was how the children of Israel came to Egypt. Joseph helped them to settle in a place called Goshen in Egypt.

## UNIT SEVEN: RUTH SERVES HER MOTHER-IN-LAW (Ruth 1-4)

The Book of Ruth tells us about a woman named Naomi who packed up and moved from Judah to Moab due to a terrible famine that was affecting her family. She and her husband, Elimelech moved to Moab with their two sons, Mahlon and Chilion. In Moab these two sons got married to Moabite women named, Ruth and Orpah respectively.

Tragically, Naomi lost her husband and two sons. Broken and empty, Naomi decided to move back to Bethlehem in Judah since there was no more famine there. Orpah kissed her mother-in-law good-bye but Ruth chose to go with her mother-in-law, Naomi to Judah since she had also lost her husband. Ruth said to Naomi, *"Wherever you go I will go, and where you lodge, I will lodge, your people will be my people and your God will be my God, where you die, I will die and there will I be buried"*(Ruth 1:16). Keep in mind that Ruth was a Moabite woman, and she was now moving to Judah as a foreigner. This was a big deal in their culture, but she was committed to Naomi as her daughter-in-law, and she wanted to follow after the God of Israel.

While in Judah, Ruth began to pick up grain in the field of Boaz, a close relative of Elimelech, her deceased father-in-law. God worked out an amazing plan for Boaz to take Ruth as his wife, give her a child, and provide for her and Naomi. What's remarkable about this plan was that Boaz was qualified as a "kinsman redeemer" to take her as his wife in a LEVIRATE MARRIAGE.

What in the world is a "kinsman redeemer" or a levirate marriage, you may ask? Well, they had a custom in those days, based upon Deuteronomy 25:5–6, that directed that a relative of a man who dies should marry that man's widow in order to perpetuate his lineage through this woman.

According to God's remarkable sovereignty, it turned out that Boaz was a relative to Ruth's husband who had passed away; so, he was qualified to marry her and perpetuate his lineage. So, even in the midst of Ruth and Naomi's awful affliction, God still had a plan for them. Ruth and Boaz had a son called Obed who became the grandfather of King David.

## SUMMARY

1. Joseph faithfully served his family, Potiphar, the king of Egypt and the world.
2. Ruth also lived a selfless life of service to Naomi her mother in-law.
3. Joseph received the blessing of becoming a leader in a foreign land.
4. Ruth, a foreigner, became a part of the lineage of Jesus (as the great- grandmother to King David).

## MORAL LESSONS

1. We should always make effort to ensure that we render services faithfully, loyally and also be accountable just like Joseph.
2. It takes courage to serve. So we must be courageous as seen in the decision of Ruth.
3. As children of God, we should be attentive enough to be able to identify those who need our assistance so as to help them.
4. Jealousy hinders prosperity. We should abstain from Jealousy; we should not be like Joseph's brothers.

## EVALUATION/REVISION QUESTIONS

1. What is service?
2. Narrate the story of Ruth's faithfulness in her service to her mother-in-law.
3. Identify three blessings derived from rendering faithful service.
4. What moral lesson did you learn from the services rendered by Joseph and Ruth?

# THEME FOURTEEN:
# CALL TO REPENTANCE

## INTRODUCTION

Despite man's sin, God is not willing that any should perish, but that all should come to repentance (II Peter 3:9). The Lord is pleading with us His people to repent and return to our rightful place, worshiping Him as His chosen people. Like a loving Father with a wayward child, God's heart breaks for His rebellious people. In His justice, He cannot withhold His judgment, and in His grace, He calls us to repentance.

## UNIT ONE: MEANING OF REPENTANCE

Repentance simply means being sorry for something you have done wrong. It includes turning away from sin and turning to God for forgiveness. It is a call to conversion from self-love, self-trust, and self-assertion to obedient trust and self-commitment to God. Repentance is motivated by love from God and the sincere desire to obey his commandments. The Lord has declared that "No unclean thing can inherit the kingdom to heaven. Our sins makes us unclean – unworthy to return and dwell in the presence of our heavenly Father.

Repentance also involves feeling sorry for wrong done to our fellow men. Sometimes, due to greed or jealousy people disagree, quarrel and offend one another. This leads to break in relationship. There becomes a need to restore broken relationship so that we can live in peace and harmony. It is an act of repentance for one to be remorseful for one's wrongful act and ask for forgiveness so as to restore broken relationship. Many people in the Bible repented of their sins after erring. Examples of such people are King David, the people of Nineveh, the Prodigal son, Zacchaeus etc.

<table>
<tr><td>

**UNIT TWO:**
</td><td>

## KING DAVID OBEYS GOD'S CALL TO REPENTANCE (2 Samuel. 12:7-13; Psalm. 51:1-9)
</td></tr>
</table>

King David sinned against God when he took Uriah's wife, got her pregnant and put her husband, Uriah to death. God sent Prophet Nathan to warn David about his sin. David humbly agreed that he had sinned against God. He fasted, tore his clothes and lay on the bare floor, pleading for God's mercy and forgiveness. Even when the child born out of David's adulterous act died, David accepted it as the will of God. David's sign of repentance could be seen in Psalm 51.

<table>
<tr><td>

**UNIT THREE:**
</td><td>

## ZACCHAEUS OBEYS GOD'S CALL TO REPENTANCE (LUKE 19:1-9)
</td></tr>
</table>

Zacchaeus was a dishonest man whose curiosity led him to Jesus Christ and salvation. Ironically, his name means "pure" or "innocent" in Hebrew. As a chief tax collector for the vicinity of Jericho, Zacchaeus was an employee of the Roman Empire. Under the Roman system, men bid on those positions, pledging to raise a certain amount of money. Anything they raised over that amount was their personal profit.

Luke says Zacchaeus was a wealthy man, so he must have extorted a great deal from the people and encouraged his subordinates to do so as well. Jesus was passing through Jericho one day, but because Zacchaeus was a short man, he could not see over the crowd. He ran ahead and climbed a sycamore tree to get a better view. To his astonishment and delight, Jesus stopped, looked up, and ordered Zacchaeus to come down because he would stay at his house.

The crowd, however, muttered that Jesus would be socializing with a sinner. Jews hated tax collectors because they were dishonest tools of the oppressive Roman government. The self-righteous in the crowd were especially critical of Jesus' interest in a man like Zacchaeus, but Christ was demonstrating his mission to seek and save the lost. At Jesus' call to him, Zacchaeus promised to give half his money to the poor and repay fourfold anyone he had cheated. Jesus told Zacchaeus that salvation would come to his house that day.

## UNIT FOUR: THE PEOPLE OF NINEVEH REPENTED OF THEIR SINS (Jonah 3:1-14)

Nineveh was the capital city of the Assyrian empire. It was an evil, violent city of cruelty and idolatrous disregard for Israel's God. The Lord called Jonah to go into the city of Nineveh and preach the message of repentance to them. Although the city was filled with all manner of wickedness, God in His mercy wanted to offer the people a chance to repent.

However, Jonah, having no compassion on the people and judging them worthy to receive the punishment due them, chose to rebel against the Lord's calling and sought to flee from His presence. He attempted to flee to Tarshish, but God sent a storm which troubled the ship he was travelling in. The sailor's casted lot to know who was responsible for their trouble and the Lot fell on Jonah. They threw Jonah out of the ship into the sea and he landed in the belly of a great fish (Whale). However, the Lord in His mercy delivered Jonah from the belly of the fish after Jonah cried out in prayer to the Lord, and the Lord commanded him yet a second time to go to the city of Nineveh and preach his message there. This time, Jonah heeded the voice of the Lord and surrendered to His command. He gave the people of Nineveh only Forty days to repent or face the wrath of God.

The people of Nineveh believed God's message so they decided that everyone should fast and all the people from the greatest to the least, put on sackcloth to show that they had repented. When the king of Nineveh heard about it he got up from his throne, took off his robe, put on sackcloth and sat down in ashes. He sent out a proclamation to the people of Nineveh. "This is an order from the king and his officials: No one is to eat anything all persons, cattle and sheep are forbidden to eat or drink. All persons must wear sackcloth; everyone must pray earnestly to God and must give up his wicked behavior and his evil actions. Perhaps God will change his mind, perhaps he will stop being angry and we will not die".

God saw what they did, He saw that they had given up their wicked behavior so He changed His mind and did not punish them as He had said He would.

## UNIT FIVE: JOHN THE BAPTIST CALLS FOR REPENTANCE (Luke 3:1-14).

John the Baptist, son of Zachariah and Elizabeth was one of the earliest prominent figure to have called for people's repentance from sin. John the Baptist strongly condemned the evils of men and asked them to turn from their evil ways to God and be baptized.

Crowds of people came out to John to be baptized by him. This baptism meant a new decision that the people were starting a fresh life of being honest and turning from evil.

## UNIT SIX: JESUS' CALL FOR REPENTANCE (Mark 1:14-15)

Now after John was arrested, Jesus came into Galilee, proclaiming the gospel of God, and saying, "The time is fulfilled, and the kingdom of

God is at hand; repent and believe in the gospel (Mark 1:14-15)." When Jesus spoke on repentance, when he said that we are to repent, it means to have a change of our mind, a change on our way of

thinking about things that are not in line with God. It's not just I'm not going to sin any longer." it's coming under the knowledge the truth to agree that my sin is terribly offensive to God. I don't want to sin any longer. I don't want to be opposed to God. I want to change for the better.

## UNIT SEVEN: CONSEQUENCES OF LACK OF REPENTANCE

- **The Case of Adam and Eve**(Genesis 3:6-22)

The sin of Adam and Eve and their failure to show any sign of repentance severed their relationship with their creator. They lost the comfort of Eden and had to struggle to survive.

- **The Case of Pharaoh against the Children of Israel** (Exodus 6)

Pharaoh's refusal to repent of his pride and refusal to set God's people (the Israelite) free brought different plagues, sickness, disease and death to his people

- **The Case of the Children of Eli** (1 Samuel 3:18; 4:10-21)

The failure of Eli's Children, Hophni and Phinehas to repent of their sin led to the wiping away of Eli's family and the capture of the Ark of the Covenant by their enemies, the Philistine.

- **The Case of King Saul** (1 Samuel 15:20-26, 16:14-23, 31:1-13)

King Saul's disobedience of God's command led to his rejection as king of Israel. The spirit of God left him and an evil spirit tormented him. It also led to his death and death of his three sons at Mount Gilboa.

## Summary
1. To repent is to feel sorry for one's wrong doing.
2. God forgave David, the people of Nineveh and Zacchaeus when they repented.
3. Any person who fails to repent receives condemnation and grave punishment onto himself.
4. When Jesus spoke on repentance, he meant to have a positive change in our way of life.

## Moral Lessons
1. God is very merciful.
2. To be forgiven by God, we must first repent of our wrong doing.
3. We should admit our wrong and say "I am sorry".
4. When we honestly seek for God's mercy, God is always ready to forgive us no matter how grave our sin is to Him.
5. Our failure to repent destroys our relationship with God and our fellow men.
6. If we fail to obey God's call to repentance, the consequences are punishment, suffering and death.

## Evaluation/Revision Questions
1. What is repentance?
2. Identify two (2) evidences of the repentance of the Ninevites.
3. List two acts of repentance and significance demanded by John the Baptist.
4. Give an account of the consequences surrounding Uriah's death.
5. Highlight Zaccheus call for repentance.
6. When Jesus spoke on repentance, what was he talking about.
7. List two (2) consequences of each of the following:
    I. Cultism
    II. Unchaste conduct
    III. Examination malpractices
    IV. Drunkenness
    V. Smoking
    VI. Stealing